TREASURY OF

Illustrations by Michael Adams

Nihil Obstat: Reverend Francis Vivona, S.T.M., J.C.L.

Imprimatur: Most Reverend Bishop William C. Skurla, D.D.,
Bishop of the Eparchy of Van Nuys

Date: March 21, 2007

Picture page 41 courtesy of Shrine of Saint Gianna Molla, 625 West Street Road, Warminster, PA 18974, (215) 672-3551, www.saintgianna.org; info@gianna.org.

Image of Saint Theodore Guerin courtesy of The Sisters of Providence of Saint Mary-of-the-Woods, Indiana.

Library of Congress Control Number: 2011910807
ISBN 1-936020-37-9

Fourth Printing, July, 2013

TABLE OF CONTENTS

INTRODUCTION TO WOMEN SAINTS

"Many are the women of proven worth,
but you have excelled them all."
–PROVERBS 31:29

Saint Anne

Saint Catherine of Siena

What is a saint? A saint is a person who lived a life of heroic virtue on earth, and now enjoys the fullness of God's love and glory in heaven. Whether canonized or not, each saint is someone who responded passionately to God's love and who followed Him with his or her whole heart!

Today especially girls and women need heroines whom they can look up to and follow as role models and leaders. In this book we have included nearly 100 of the best-known women saints in the Church's glorious history of martyrs and saints of God.

Pope John Paul II canonized 482 saints and beatified 1,338 others – more than any other pope in history – to give us living models of heroic virtue and to show us that holiness is in fact God's dream for **each** of his sons and daughters! The Holy Father would often say, in his deep resonant voice, "You are called to be holy!" echoing God's command to His people down through the ages.

Our current knowledge of the saints comes to us, in large degree, through the work of Father Alban Butler. Born in 1710 in England, Father Butler was one of the most prominent Catholic students during the first half of the eighteenth century. He entered the College at Douai and, after ordination, was asked to remain at the college as professor, first of philosophy, and later, of theology. During his years at Douai, Father Butler devoted himself to what would become the great work of his life, *The Lives of the Saints*, containing biographies of more than 1,600 saints! Many of the stories told in this book are the edited versions of Father Butler's original work.

Saint Josephine Bakhita

Blessed Teresa of Calcutta

Many saints are known for certain patronages – some for numerous patronages – and we have chosen one of those for each saint. For some saints, we found no patronage, and in those cases we chose a patronage based on their life and tradition.

In the end, there is only one Master. All the rest of us are invited to follow Him. May these lives of the saints, heroines of our faith, inspire all of us to love Jesus more fervently and follow Him more closely, day by day.

SAINT AGATHA

Patroness of Nurses

Feast Day: February 5

Saint Agatha was born in Sicily, of rich and noble parents – a child of benediction from the first, for she was promised to her parents before her birth, and consecrated from her earliest infancy to God. In the midst of dangers and temptations she served Christ in purity of body and soul, and she died for the love of chastity. Quintanus, who governed Sicily under the Emperor Decius, had heard the rumor of her beauty and wealth, and he made the laws against the Christians a pretext for summoning her from Palermo to Catania, where he was at the time. "O Jesus Christ!" she cried, as she set out on this dreaded journey, "all that I am is Thine; preserve me against the tyrant."

Our Lord did indeed preserve one who had given herself so utterly to Him. He kept her pure and undefiled while she was imprisoned for a whole month under charge of an evil woman. He gave her strength to reply to the offer of her life and safety, if she would but consent to sin, "Christ alone is my life and my salvation."

When Quintanus turned from passion to cruelty, and cut off her breasts, Our Lord sent the Prince of His Apostles to heal Agatha. And when, after she had been rolled naked upon potsherds, she asked that her torments might be ended, her Spouse heard her prayer and took Saint Agatha to Himself.

SAINT AGNES

Patroness of Young Women

Feast Day: January 21

Saint Agnes was only 12 years old when she was led to the altar of Minerva at Rome and commanded to offer incense to the pagan gods. Instead, she raised her hands to Christ, her Spouse, and made the sign of the life-giving cross. Agnes did not shrink when she was bound hand and foot, though the ropes slipped from her young hands, and the pagans around were moved to tears. The bonds were not needed for her, and she hastened gladly to the place of her torture.

When the judge saw that pain had no terrors for her, he inflicted an insult worse than death: her clothes were stripped off, and she had to stand in the street before a pagan crowd; yet even this did not daunt her. "Christ," she said, "will guard His own." And so He did.

Agnes proclaimed, "Christ is my Spouse: He chose me first, and His I will be." For a moment she stood erect in prayer, and then bowed her neck to the sword. At one stroke her head was severed, and the angels bore the pure soul of Saint Agnes to Paradise.

One victim, but a twin martyrdom, to modesty and religion; Saint Agnes preserved her virginity and gained a martyr's crown.

–Saint Ambrose of Milan

SAINT ALICE

Patroness of Cheerful Suffering

Feast Day: June 15

Alice was born in Schaerbeck, a suburb of Brussels, Belgium, in the early 13th century. She was a frail child with a charming personality. At an early age she entered the convent of Camera Sanctae Mariae and stayed there for the rest of her life.

The sisters educated Alice in the things of the world and the things of God, and she did well in both areas. They loved her especially for her humility. Suddenly, Alice was struck with a dread disease: leprosy!

Alice spent the rest of her life in isolation. Even so, her cheerful spirit in this dark night of the soul and body brought great strength to her congregation. Her greatest joy was to receive our Lord in the Holy Eucharist. Because leprosy was contagious, she was not allowed to drink from the cup. One day Jesus Himself appeared to Alice and assured her that those who receive the Host received both His body and blood, for "Where there is part, there is also the whole."

On June 11, 1249, Sister Alice received the Anointing of the Sick, and perceived she would die in a year. Her suffering increased, and she even lost her sight due to the disease. However she offered her suffering for all, especially the souls in purgatory, and experienced ecstasies and revelations. On June 10, 1250, Saint Alice went home to Jesus. Alice is also known as Saint Adelaide of La Cambre.

SAINT ANASTASIA

Patroness of Widows

Feast Day: December 25

Anastasia was the daughter of a wealthy Roman pagan and a Christian mother, who raised her secretly to love Jesus and follow His Gospel.

Anastasia was married to Publius, a Roman pagan, who one day discovered her helping Christian prisoners. He confined her to her house and treated her poorly. Anastasia rejoiced that she had been counted worthy to suffer for the love of Jesus.

Publius left for a journey after ordering his slaves to mistreat Anastasia; however, he died on the journey and she continued her ministry to the prisoners, one of whom was Saint Chrysogonus. He had been in prison a year, sharing the faith with his fellow prisoners, and Anastasia helped him greatly.

In 303, Saint Chrysogonus was beheaded by the order of Emperor Diocletian, but Anastasia continued helping others. One day she wept bitterly as she realized that all the believers she knew had been executed. The Prefect Florus then arrested her also, and commanded her to worship false gods. When Anastasia refused, she was sent to an official named Upian, who tried to get her to sin, and was struck dead on the spot.

Florus then tried to starve and sink Anastasia, but the Lord delivered her. Finally Florus executed Anastasia in Dalmatia, on December 25th, 304. We remember Saint Anastasia today in the First Eucharistic Prayer of the Mass.

SAINT ANGELA MERICI

Patroness of the Sick and Disabled

Feast Day: January 27

Angela Merici, founder of the first teaching congregation of women in the Church, was born at Desenzano, Italy, in 1474. From her earliest years, she kept the strictest guard over her chastity. While yet a young girl, she lost her parents, and set out for the desert to lead a life of penance; but being prevented by an uncle, she devoted herself to prayer and fasting at home. At 15, she entered the Third Order of Saint Francis of Assisi.

During a pilgrimage to the Holy Land, Angela suddenly went blind. She insisted on continuing her trip, visiting the shrines and praying at the sites. On the way home, she was cured!

In 1535, deeply bothered by the ignorance of poor girls who had neither education nor hope, Angela gathered a group of girls and founded the Institute of Saint Ursula to teach children. She wanted to re-Christianize family life through the education of future wives and mothers. She courageously sought a new way to evangelize and help those in need around her. She told her companions, "You have a greater need to serve than the poor have of your service."

After her death in 1540, Angela's Ursuline order grew and spread throughout the world. Saint Angela Merici was canonized in 1807, and today her body is incorrupt.

"Mothers of children, even if they have a thousand, carry each and every one fixed in their hearts."

–Saint Angela Merici

SAINT ANNE

Patroness of Grandmothers

Feast Day: July 26

Saint Anne, the spouse of Saint Joachim, was chosen by God to be the mother of Mary, His own blessed Mother on earth. Joachim and Anne, of the royal house of David, devoted themselves to prayer and good works. Unfortunately, they were childless, a bitter misfortune among the Jews.

When Anne grew old, Mary was born, the fruit rather of grace than of nature, and the child more of God than of man. With the birth of Mary, the aged Anne began a new life: she watched her every movement with reverent tenderness, and felt herself hourly sanctified by the presence of her immaculate child. Anne and Joachim had vowed to give God their daughter, and to Him Anne gave her back.

Mary was three years old when her mother and father led her up the Temple steps, saw her pass by herself into the inner sanctuary, and then saw her no more. Thus was Saint Anne left childless in her old age, and deprived of her purest earthly joy just when she needed it most. She humbly adored the divine Will, and began again to watch and pray, until God called her to unending rest with the Father and the Spouse of Mary in the home of Mary's Child.

SAINT APOLLONIA

Patroness of Dentists and Toothaches

Feast Day: February 9

Apollonia was a virgin who lived in Alexandria, Egypt, and a deaconess in the church that met there. In the year 249, during the reign of Emperor Phillip, a local poet agitated the people of Alexandria, causing an uprising against the Christians. A mob seized two Christians – an old man named Metrius and a woman named Quinta – and put them to death. They then ruined the homes of some other believers, and finally seized Apollonia, described by Saint Dionysius of Alexandria as being a deaconess advanced in years and held in high esteem.

The men struck Apollonia in the mouth repeatedly, breaking all her teeth. They then dragged her outside the city gates to a great bonfire. The mob gave Apollonia a moment of freedom to reconsider her choice, and commanded her to worship their pagan gods. Suddenly Apollonia leaped into the fire and was burned to death! Thus she voluntarily accepted the death prepared for her. Saint Augustine compared her sacrifice to that of Samson in the Old Testament, who, with the help of God, pulled down the pillars of the Temple in Jerusalem, killing himself and all of his Philistine captors.

Many churches and altars were dedicated to Saint Apollonia in Rome; today, all that remains is a square that is still called the "Piazza Santa Apollonia."

Saint Apollonia, please pray for us.

SAINT BARBARA

Patroness of Construction Workers

Feast Day: December 4

Saint Barbara was brought up a heathen. A tyrannical father, Dioscorus, kept her jealously secluded in a lonely tower which he had built for the purpose. Here in her forced solitude, she gave herself to prayer and study, and contrived to receive instruction and Baptism by stealth from a Christian priest.

Dioscorus, on discovering his daughter's conversion, was beside himself with rage. He himself denounced her before the civil tribunal. Barbara was horribly tortured, and at last was beheaded by her own father, who, mercilessly to the last, acted as her executioner.

God, however, speedily punished her persecutors. While her soul was being borne by angels to Paradise, a flash of lightning struck Dioscorus, and he was hurried before the judgment-seat of God. Because of this, Saint Barbara is often invoked during thunderstorms and lightning.

Through the intercession of Saint Barbara, may God, who loves us, protect us from a sudden or accidental death and help us always be ready to meet Him. Let us pray that we will be able to receive the anointing of the sick and the gift of Viaticum, our final Holy Communion, before we die and go to meet the Lord.

SAINT BEATRICE OF SILVA

Patroness of Prisoners

Feast Day: September 1

Beatrice was born in Morocco of Portugese parents, in 1424. She had a great love for Our Blessed Mother Mary. Beatrice served Princess Isabel of Portugal and traveled with her to Spain when Isabel married John II of Castille. However, Beatrice grew weary of court life and entered a convent at Toledo.

Beatrice never took final vows, and at the age of 60 she founded a new contemplative community, the Congregation of the Immaculate Conception of the Blessed Virgin Mary. Her rule emphasized silence and obedience, humility, and a deep love for all. Saint Beatrice died in Toledo on September 1, 1490, and Pope Paul VI canonized her in 1976.

Saint Beatrice tried always to be open to God and His Will for her life, even when it meant waiting and seeking different possibilities. Her obedience was rewarded. After her death, Pope Alexander VI placed her Congregation under the Franciscan Order and her nuns are now known as the Conceptionist Poor Clares.

"For above everything else there flourishes among them that excelling virtue of mutual and continual charity, which so binds their wills into one that, though forty or fifty of them dwell together in one place, agreement in likes and dislikes molds one spirit in them out of many."

–THOMAS OF CELANO, FRANCISCAN BIOGRAPHER, ON THE LIFE OF THE EARLY FRANCISCANS.

SAINT BERNADETTE SOUBIROUS

Patroness of the Sick

Feast Day: April 16

Bernadette Soubirous was born in Lourdes, France, on January 7, 1844. A severe asthma sufferer, Bernadette was living with her parents and family in a converted jail, when on February 11, 1858, the Blessed Virgin Mary appeared to her in a cave on the banks of the Gave River near Lourdes. Crowds began to gather and grow as Bernadette reported further visits from the Virgin, from February 18 through March 4. The civil authorities tried to frighten Bernadette into recanting her accounts, but she remained faithful to the vision.

On February 25, at Mary's request, Bernadette dug at a spot near the grotto, from which a spring emerged, with healing waters. On March 25, Mary told Bernadette, "I am the Immaculate Conception." She also requested that a church be built on the site. Many authorities tried to stop the work, but the fame of the visions reached Empress Eugenie of France, wife of Napoleon III, and construction went forward.

In 1866, Bernadette joined the Sisters of Notre Dame in Nevers. She died there on April 16, 1879, still giving the same account of her visions. With over 200 million pilgrims since 1858, Lourdes has become one of the major pilgrimage destinations in the world. Pope Pius XI canonized Saint Bernadette in 1933, and her body lies incorrupt at Nevers.

SAINT BRIDGET OF SWEDEN

Co-Patroness of Europe

Feast Day: July 23

Bridget was born of the Swedish royal family in 1304. At the age of seven, she began receiving visions of Christ crucified, which spurred her on to serve others in love. At the age of 12, Bridget lost her mother, and was married at 13 to Prince Ulpho of Sweden. Bridget became the mother of eight children, one of whom was Saint Catherine of Sweden.

Bridget counseled and guided King Magnus and Queen Blanche of Sweden. Widowed at 42, she received a series of the most sublime revelations, all of which she scrupulously submitted to the judgment of her confessor. In 1346, Bridget founded the religious order now known as the Bridgetines.

In 1350, Bridget journeyed to Rome, where she advised priest and pope alike. Later on, at Our Lord's command, she made a pilgrimage to the Holy Land, where He instructed her in the sacred mysteries amid the very scenes of His Passion. Bridget wrote a book of prayers concerning the revelations, which is popular to this day. Finally, saddened by the death of her son, Bridget died in 1373 in Rome, and was canonized by Pope Boniface IX in 1391.

God drew Saint Bridget to Himself and then sent her to live a holy life in the middle of all the activity and business of the world. In 1999, Pope John Paul II named Saint Bridget, Saint Catherine of Siena, and Saint Edith Stein as co-patronesses of all Europe.

SAINT BRIGID OF IRELAND

Patroness of Sailors

Feast Day: February 1

Brigid was probably born at Faughart near Dundalk, Louth, Ireland, in 453. Her parents were baptized by Saint Patrick, with whom she developed a close friendship. According to legend, her father was Dubhthach, an Irish chieftain of Lienster, and her mother, Brocca, was a slave at his court. Even as a young girl, Brigid showed an interest for a religious life and took the veil in her youth from Saint Macaille at Croghan. She probably was professed by Saint Mel of Armagh, who is believed to have conferred abbatial authority on her.

Brigid settled with seven of her virgins at the foot of Croghan Hill for a time and about the year 468, followed Saint Mel to Meath. About the year 470 she founded a double monastery at Cill-Dara (Kildare) and was Abbess of the convent, the first in Ireland. The foundation developed into a center of learning and spirituality, and around it grew up the Cathedral city of Kildare.

Brigid founded a school of art in Kildare and its illuminated manuscripts became famous, notably the Book of Kildare, which was praised as one of the finest of all illuminated Irish manuscripts before its disappearance three centuries ago. Brigid was one of the most remarkable women of her times, and despite the numerous legendary, extravagant, and even fantastic miracles attributed to her, there is no doubt that her extraordinary spirituality, boundless charity, and compassion for those in distress were real.

Saint Brigid of Ireland died at Kildare on February 1, 525.

SAINT CATHERINE DEL RICCI

Patroness of Bodily Ills

Feast Day: February 13

Alessandra del Ricci was born April 23, 1522, in Florence, Italy. After her mother's early death, Alessandra was raised by her Godmother, who taught her to spend time in solitary prayer to Our Lord. At 6, Alessandra entered convent school, and became a Dominican in 1536, taking the name Catherine.

In the first years of her religious life, her sisters, who misunderstood God's gifts to Catherine of ecstasy and holiness, misjudged Catherine. But her true holiness, humility, and gift of administration convinced them, and they appointed her as sub-prioress and prioress until her death.

In Lent of 1542, Catherine experienced for the first time the "Ecstasy of the Passion of Jesus" at noon every Thursday until 4 PM on Friday, as first the wounds from Christ's scourging, then those of His crown of thorns, would appear on her body. At the end she would be covered with wounds and her shoulder actually indented from the weight of Jesus' cross.

Crowds of people came to see Catherine; skeptics and sinners were converted at the sight. Due to the disruption of the convent life, the nuns asked that the wounds would be less visible, and in 1554, the ecstasies ceased. Three future popes were among the many who sought Catherine's prayers and guidance. She died in 1590, and Pope Benedict XIV canonized Saint Catherine del Ricci in 1746.

SAINT CATHERINE LABOURÉ

Patroness of Architects

Feast Day: November 25

Catherine Labouré was born on May 2, 1806, and at age 24 she entered the Daughters of Charity, in Paris, France. On the night of July 18, 1830, suddenly an angel awoke Catherine, telling her to go to the chapel. The Blessed Mother appeared there, speaking to Catherine and asking her to help spread devotion to her Immaculate Conception. Catherine agreed, and Our Lady appeared to her again, directing her to have a medal struck with her image and the words, "O Mary, conceived without sin, pray for us who have recourse to thee" on one side, and the Hearts of Jesus and Mary on the other. Our Lady told Catherine that wearers of the medal, which came to be known as the Miraculous Medal, would receive great graces.

Sister Catherine shared the vision with her confessor, who saw to it that the medal was made and distributed, all the while keeping Catherine's identity a secret. 45 years later, when she was near death, Catherine revealed her secret and told her superior everything.

Saint Catherine Labouré died on December 31, 1876, and her funeral Mass was filled with songs of joy and celebration, for this true daughter of Jesus and Mary had gone home at last!

SAINT CATHERINE OF ALEXANDRIA

Patroness of Philosophers and Preachers

Feast Day: November 25

Catherine was a noble virgin of Alexandria who converted to Christianity after receiving a vision. At 18, she debated the Faith with 50 pagan philosophers – and converted them! The tyrant Maximus martyred all of them, and then ordered Catherine to be imprisoned and scourged. In prison Catherine preached and debated with the emperor's wife and 200 of his soldiers, and they too received Christ as their Savior, and were martyred.

The enraged Maximus then ordered Catherine to be executed on a spiked wheel. It shattered at her touch, and he beheaded Catherine in 305 AD. Angels are said to have carried her body to a monastery at the foot of Mount Sinai.

Devotion to Saint Catherine spread during the Crusades, and students, teachers, librarians, and lawyers especially asked for her patronage. During the infamous Black Plague of Europe in the fourteenth century, Saint Catherine was considered one of the Fourteen Holy Helpers, and Catholics prayed for her intercession to help end the devastation and death. In 1349 the plague ceased.

The constancy that the saints display in their courageous martyrdom cannot be isolated from their previous lives, but is their natural sequence. If we wish to emulate their perseverance, let us first imitate their fidelity to grace.

SAINT CATHERINE OF SIENA

Patroness of Purity

Feast Day: April 29

Catherine of Siena was born the daughter of humble Italian weavers in 1347. As a child, she loved to pray and even had visions of angels. At seven years old, Catherine made a vow of virginity, and at 15, she entered the Third Order of Saint Dominic, remaining in her father's shop, where she united a life of active charity with contemplative prayer.

Under Christ's command, Catherine traveled through Italy, bringing people back to obedience to the Pope, and winning hardened souls to God. Through her influence Pope Gregory XI returned from Avignon to Rome, and she exhorted him to contribute, by all possible means, toward the peace of Italy.

In 1378, Catherine saw with sorrow the beginning of the Great Schism with two and then three popes reigning simultaneously. She wrote to the cardinals who were the cause of it and to several princes, in order to avert the terrible evil.

Saint Catherine of Siena, mystic, stigmatist, visionary, miracle worker, counselor, and writer, died April 29, 1380, at the age of 33. Pope Pius II canonized her in 1461 and on October 4, 1970, Pope Paul VI declared Saint Catherine of Siena a Doctor of the Church.

SAINT CATHERINE OF SWEDEN

Patroness of Protection against Abortion, Miscarriages

Feast Day: March 24

Catherine of Sweden was born in 1330 as the fourth child of Prince Ulpho and Saint Bridget. At seven years of age, her parents placed Catherine in the convent of Risburgh, and she was educated in piety under the care of the holy abbess. Being very beautiful, she was, by her father, contracted in marriage to Egard, a young nobleman of great virtue; but Catherine persuaded him to join with her in making a mutual vow of perpetual chastity and continence. The happy couple, having but one heart and one desire, encouraged each other to prayer, mortification, and works of charity.

After her father's death, Catherine, out of devotion to the Passion of Christ and to the relics of the martyrs, accompanied her mother to Rome in 1348. Her husband Egard died soon thereafter and the two women lived penitential lives of devotion, leading pilgrimages to holy sites, including Jerusalem. They also cared for and instructed the poor. Many men sought Catherine's hand in marriage, but she remained true to her vocation.

After Saint Bridget's death at Rome in 1373, Catherine returned her mother's body to Sweden, and was elected superior of the Bridgettine order her mother had founded. Abbess Catherine died March 24th, 1381. All of Sweden mourned her, as they had her mother. Pope Innocent VIII canonized Saint Catherine of Sweden in 1484.

SAINT CECILIA

Patroness of Musicians

Feast Day: November 22

Cecilia, a rich, beautiful, and noble Roman maiden, had vowed her virginity to God. When her parents had her married to Valerian, hearing heavenly music in her heart, Cecilia told him that an angel, whom he could see once he was purified, always accompanied her.

Valerian received Baptism, saw the angel, and helped convert his brother Tiburtius. Both men were arrested for burying martyred Christians, and were martyred themselves.

Cecilia buried Valerian and his brother, for which she was also arrested. "Do you not know," was her answer to the threats of the Roman prefect, "that I am the bride of my Lord Jesus Christ?" He ordered her to be suffocated in a hot-air bath, heated seven times over. But "the flames had no power over her body, neither was a hair of her head singed."

The executioner sent to behead Cecilia struck the three blows which the law allowed, and left her still alive. For two days and nights Cecilia lay with her head half severed on the pavement of her bath, fully sensible, and joyfully awaiting her crown; on the third the agony was over, and in 177 the virgin Saint gave back her pure spirit to Christ.

Saint Cecilia is the patroness of music, singers, and musicians.

SAINT CHRISTINA

Patroness of Millers, Archers, and Mariners

Feast Day: July 24

Saint Christina was born in the third century, the daughter of Urban, a rich and powerful Roman governor. Her pagan father had a number of golden idols, which Christina broke into pieces and gave to the poor. Infuriated by this, Urban had his daughter whipped and thrown into a dungeon. Christina remained unshaken in her faith. Urban then had her body torn by iron hooks, and fastened her to a rack over a fire. But God watched over His servant and turned the flames upon the onlookers. Urban then had the executioner seize Christina, tie a heavy stone about her neck; and cast her into the lake of Bolsena, but an angel saved her, and her father died suddenly.

The judge who succeeded her father also ordered inhuman torments for Christina, and he likewise died suddenly. Finally, a third judge, Julian, cried, "Adore the gods, or I will put you to death!" Christina survived a burning furnace, where she remained, unhurt, for five days. By the power of Christ she overcame the serpents among which she was thrown; then her tongue was cut out, and afterwards, she was pierced with arrows.

Saint Christina died a martyr at Tyro, a city which formerly stood on an island in the lake of Bolsena in Italy, but was long since swallowed up by the waters. Her relics are now at Palermo in Sicily.

SAINT CLARE

Patroness of Television

Feast Day: August 11

As a young girl, Clare imitated her mother's love for the poor of her native Assisi. Inspired by the preaching of Saint Francis, who sang enthusiastically of His Lord Jesus and Lady Poverty, Clare gave her life to Jesus at 19, allowing Francis to cut off her beautiful hair and invest her with the Franciscan habit.

Clare founded the Poor Clares, who wore no shoes, ate no meat, lived in a poor house, and kept silent. Yet they were very happy, because Our Lord was close to them all the time.

In 1244, Saracen soldiers came to attack the Poor Clare convent in Assisi. Although very sick, Clare had her sisters carry her to the wall and she placed the Blessed Sacrament in the enemies' view, while she begged God for help. A child's voice answered, "I will keep you always in My care." A sudden fright struck the attackers, who fled for their lives!

Clare greatly aided Saint Francis with his new order, carrying on his spirit in the Franciscans after his death. Since she was too ill to attend Mass, an image of the service appeared on her cell wall – hence her patronage of television! Clare died on August 11, 1253. Pope Alexander IV canonized Saint Clare of Assisi in 1255, and today her body lies incorrupt in the church of Santa Chiara in Assisi.

SAINT CLARE OF MONTEFALCO

Patroness of Montefalco, Italy

Feast Day: August 17

Clare was born at Montefalco, Italy about the year 1268. Even as a child, she loved God greatly, and joined the Third Order of Saint Francis with her sister and some of their friends. In time she discerned that God was calling her to live a life wholly consecrated to Him, and she established Santa Croce, or Holy Cross, Convent in 1290. The bishop of Spoleto gave Clare and her sisters the rule of Saint Augustine as their guide.

Clare's sister Joan was selected as the abbess of the new community; after Joan's death in 1295, the nuns chose Clare to lead them. Clare served her sisters as mother, teacher, director, and friend. She heroically lived a virtuous life, ministering to the many visitors who came to see her for counsel, strength, and inspiration.

Clare once told her sisters, "If you seek the cross of Christ, take my heart; there you will find the suffering Lord." She died on August 18, 1308, at Montefalco, after which her sisters found a cross clearly imprinted on her heart. Pope Leo XIII canonized Saint Clare of Montefalco in 1881.

Saint Clare's life reminds us to seek God and to develop our friendship with Him. He will guide us into the fullness of His plans for us, which will bring about His glory, our good, and the good of all people, now and in eternity.

SAINT COLETTE

Patroness of Loss of Parents

Feast Day: March 6

Nicolette Boilet was born in 1381 in Corbie, France. After her parents' early death, she entered the Third Order of Saint Francis, and at the age of 21, she moved to a little cell near her parish church. Here Colette passed four years of extraordinary penance when Saint Francis himself appeared to her, directing her to undertake the reform of the Poor Clares.

With the Pope's approval, Colette established her reform throughout a large part of Europe, and, in spite of the most violent opposition, founded seventeen convents of the strict observance. By the same wonderful prudence she helped heal the great schism which then afflicted the Church. The Church Fathers were uncertain about how to deal with the three men who claimed to be pope. Colette, together with Saint Vincent Ferrer, helped the Fathers come to a solution, and Pope Martin V was elected, to the great good of the Church.

Saint Colette was deeply devoted to Christ's Passion. She never ceased to pray for the Church, while the devils, in turn, never ceased to assault her. Yet the virgin of Christ triumphed alike over their threats and their allurements. She died on March 6, 1447, in intercession for sinners and the Church.

If there be a true way that leads to the Everlasting Kingdom, it is most certainly that of suffering, patiently endured.

–Saint Colette

SAINT DEBORAH

Patroness of Counselors

Feast Day: November 1

Between the death of Joshua, servant of Moses, and the institution of the monarchy in Israel, God Himself governed Israel through Judges – military leaders whom He sent to help free His people from their enemies. When Israel obeyed God, He blessed them; when they disobeyed Him, He allowed pagan enemies to conquer them; when they repented, He sent leaders – Judges – to deliver them.

Deborah is one of the Judges whose story is found in the Book of Judges, Chapters 4 and 5. At that time, the Lord had allowed Israel to fall into the power of the Canaanite king, Jabin. His general, Sisera, had oppressed the people of Israel for 20 years with his 900 iron chariots. Deborah was a prophetess, who would sit under her palm tree in Bethel, near modern-day Jerusalem, and counsel the Israelites who came to her.

Deborah told Barak that God wanted him to march on Mount Tabor, with 10,000 Israelite warriors from the tribes of Naphtali and Zebulun. God promised to deliver Sisera and his army into their power. So Barak and Deborah went up to Mount Tabor, and God gave them a tremendous victory. Not one of their enemies survived.

The *Canticle of Deborah* in Judges, Chapter 5, is a great song of praise to God for this valiant woman who led Israel to victory!

SAINT DOROTHY

Patroness of Brides

Feast Day: February 6

Saint Dorothy was a young virgin, celebrated at Caesarea, where she lived, for her angelic virtue. Her parents seem to have been martyred before her in the Diocletian persecution, and when the Governor Sapricius came to Caesarea he called her before him, and sent this child of martyrs to the home where they were waiting for her.

Saint Dorothy was stretched upon the rack, and offered marriage if she would consent to sacrifice, or death if she refused. But she replied that Christ was her only Spouse, and death her desire. Dorothy was then placed in charge of two women who had fallen away from the faith, in the hope that they might pervert her; but the fire of her own heart rekindled the flame in theirs, and she led them back to Christ.

Saint Dorothy suffered in the dead of winter, and it is said that on the road to her passion a lawyer named Theophilus, who used to persecute the Christians, asked her, in mockery, to send him "apples or roses from the garden of her Spouse." The Saint granted his request, and, just before she died, a little child stood by her side bearing three apples and three roses, whom she sent to Theophilus. Theophilus repented and gave his life to Christ. He was later martyred for the Faith.

SAINT DYMPHNA

Patroness of Those Suffering Nervous and Mental Afflictions

Feast Day: May 15

Dymphna was 14 when her mother died. Her father, Damon, is said to have been afflicted with a mental illness, brought on by his grief. He sent messengers throughout his town and other lands to find some woman of noble birth, resembling his wife, who would be willing to marry him.

When no woman could be found, Damon's evil advisers told him to marry his own daughter. Dymphna fled from her castle together with Saint Gerebran, her confessor and two other friends. Damon found them in Belgium. He gave orders that the priest's head be cut off. Then Damon tried to persuade his daughter to return to Ireland with him. When she refused, he drew his sword and struck off her head. She was only 15 years of age.

Saint Dymphna received the crown of martyrdom in defense of her purity about the year 620. She is the patron of those suffering from nervous and mental afflictions. Many miracles have taken place at her shrine, built on the spot where she was buried in Gheel, Belgium.

SAINT ELIZABETH ANN SETON

Patroness of Converts

Feast Day: January 4

Elizabeth Bayley Seton was the first native-born American to be canonized by the Catholic Church. Born into an influential Episcopalian family in 1774, Elizabeth grew up in the "cream" of New York society. She read prolifically, everything from the Bible to contemporary novels.

In spite of her background, Elizabeth's early life was quiet, simple, and often lonely. As she grew older, the Bible was to become her continual instruction, support, and comfort; she would continue to love the Scriptures for the rest of her life.

In 1794, Elizabeth married the wealthy young William Seton. Tragically, within a decade, William's business and health failed and he died of tuberculosis, leaving Elizabeth a widow with their five children at the age of 29.

Elizabeth, drawn to the Real Presence of Christ in the Eucharist, became a Roman Catholic in 1805. At the invitation of Archbishop John Carroll of Baltimore, she opened the first free Catholic school for girls, Saint Joseph's Academy, initiating the parochial school system in America. In 1809, Elizabeth founded the Sisters of Charity to help run the school.

By 1818, in addition to their first school, Mother Seton and her sisters had established two orphanages and another school. Today six groups of sisters trace their origins to Mother Seton's initial foundation.

For the last three years of her life, Elizabeth felt that God was getting ready to call her, and this gave her joy. She died in 1821 at the age of 46, only 16 years after becoming a Catholic. Mother Elizabeth Seton was canonized on September 14, 1975.

SAINT ELIZABETH OF HUNGARY

Patroness of the Homeless

Feast Day: November 17

Elizabeth was the daughter of the king of Hungary, and a niece of Saint Hedwig. She was betrothed in infancy to Louis of Thuringia, and brought up in his father's court. Not content with receiving daily numbers of poor in her palace, and relieving all in distress, she built several hospitals, where she served the sick, dressing the most repulsive sores with her own hands.

Once as Elizabeth was carrying in the folds of her mantle some provisions for the poor, she met her husband returning from a hunt. Astonished to see her bending under the weight of her burden, he opened the mantle which she kept pressed against her, and found in it nothing but beautiful red and white roses, although it was not the season for flowers. Bidding her pursue her way, he took one of the marvelous roses, and kept it all his life.

On her husband's death Saint Elizabeth was cruelly driven from her palace, and forced to wander through the streets with her little children, a prey to hunger and cold; but she welcomed all her sufferings, and continued to be the mother of the poor, converting many by her holy life.

Saint Elizabeth of Hungary died in 1231, at the age of 24.

Before Elizabeth's death I heard her confession. When I asked her what should be done about her goods and possessions, she replied that anything which seemed to be hers belonged to the poor. ... When all this had been decided, she received the body of our Lord. ... Then, she devoutly commended to God all who were sitting near her, and as if falling into a gentle sleep, she died.

—FROM A LETTER BY CONRAD OF MARBURG,
SPIRITUAL DIRECTOR OF SAINT ELIZABETH OF HUNGARY

SAINT ELIZABETH OF PORTUGAL

Patroness of Difficult Marriages

Feast Day: July 4

Elizabeth, also known as Queen Isabella of Portugal, was born in 1271, the daughter of Pedro III of Aragon, and named after her great aunt, Saint Elizabeth of Hungary. At 12 years of age she was given in marriage to Denis, King of Portugal, and from a holy child became a saintly wife. She attended Mass and prayed the Divine Office daily, and carried out faithfully all the duties of her state.

Elizabeth suffered due to her husband's infidelity and abuse, yet she prayed for his conversion and remained loyal. In 1323 her son Alfonso rebelled against his father, and Elizabeth rode onto the battlefield to reconcile them. Her patience, and the sweetness with which she even cherished the children of her rivals, completely won the king from his evil ways, and he became a devoted husband and a truly Christian king.

Elizabeth built many charitable institutions and religious houses, including a convent of Poor Clares. After her husband's death, she entered the Third Order of Saint Francis, and went to live with the Poor Clares in Coimbra. She spent the rest of her life in penance and almsgiving. Saint Elizabeth of Portugal died on July 4, 1336, while seeking to make peace among her children.

In daily Mass Saint Elizabeth found strength to bear with hardship and win the final victory of love.

SAINT EMILIANA

Patroness of Single Laywomen

Feast Day: December 24

Emiliana was the sister of the Roman Senator, Gordianus, and his wife, Saint Sylvia. Her sister was Saint Trasilla. The two sisters were the aunts of Pope Saint Gregory the Great, and lived in sixth-century Rome.

Emiliana and her sister Trasilla lived consecrated lives of virginity, prayer, and self-denial as hermits in their father's home. The sisters encouraged each other by word and deed to keep on seeking the Lord and living holy lives. It is said that Emiliana prayed so much that her knees and elbows actually locked into the praying position!

The two sisters enjoyed God's peace and love in their hearts and lives until their time came to depart this life. Saint Gregory relates that one night, Pope Saint Felix, the sisters' great-grandfather, appeared to Trasilla in a vision saying, "Come; I will receive you into this habitation of light." Trasilla fell ill with a fever the next day and she died on Christmas Eve, crying, "Make way! Jesus is coming!"

A few days later Saint Trasilla appeared to Emiliana, and invited her to join her in heaven for the Feast of the Epiphany. Saint Emiliana died January 5, in the year 550.

Saint Emiliana's relics, along with those of Saint Trasilla and their mother, Saint Sylvia, are preserved at the Oratory of Saint Andrew on the Celian Hill in Rome.

SAINT ESTHER

Patroness of Godly Rulers

Feast Day: November 1

The Old Testament Book of Esther tells the marvelous story of a young Israelite girl, Hadassah, from the tribe of Benjamin. She was exiled, with all Jews, to the land of Persia, and there was called Esther – a star. Esther was raised by her mother and her uncle Mordecai, a servant of King Xerxes, around 500 BC.

King Xerxes had divorced his wife, Queen Vashti, due to her disobedience and dishonor. He then married Esther, who was beautiful and lovely to behold. Mordecai had counseled his niece Esther to not reveal her nationality to the king.

King Xerxes' top official was a man named Haman, who had plotted to have all the Jews in the Persian Empire destroyed because Mordecai refused to bow down to him. Mordecai begged Esther to help. It was forbidden for anyone, including the Queen, to appear unsummoned before the king, so she and all the Israelites fasted and prayed for three days as Esther pleaded, "Be mindful of us, O LORD. Manifest yourself in the time of our distress and give me courage." (ESTHER C:23)

Esther bravely went before the King, who accepted her and heard the whole matter. He decreed that Haman be hung and that the Jews be spared from the destruction he had ordered. God spared His people Israel through the intervention of Queen Esther and the deliverance is celebrated to this day as the Jewish feast of Purim.

SAINT FAUSTINA

Patroness of Devotion to the Divine Mercy

Feast Day: October 5

Helena Kowalska was born in Poland in 1905. At 19, she devoted her life as Sister Faustina to the education of troubled young women. Soon thereafter, Jesus appeared to her with the message of Divine mercy with which He wanted her to "run throughout the world."

Jesus asked Sister Faustina to be merciful, and to encourage others to trust in Him, saying "I desire to heal aching mankind, pressing it to my merciful heart." He asked that she have a painting done of His Divine mercy, portraying the red and white rays of His mercy emanating from His heart, with the inscription: *Jesus, I trust in You.* Sister Faustina's entire life, like Jesus' life, was to be a sacrifice – a life lived for others.

Sister Faustina's devotion to Mary, the Eucharist, and the sacrament of Reconciliation gave her strength to offer her sufferings to God for the Church and those in special need, especially great sinners and the dying.

Sister Faustina, the cheerful, humble nun who brought Jesus' message of mercy to His world, died from tuberculosis in 1938. Pope John Paul II canonized Saint Faustina on Divine Mercy Sunday, April 30, 2000.

SAINT FRANCES OF ROME

Patroness of Automobile Drivers

Feast Day: March 9

Frances was born at Rome in 1384, to a wealthy family. Her father overruled her desire to become a nun, and had her married at the age of 12 to Lorenzo Ponziano, a Roman noble. While spending her days in prayer, she attended promptly to every household duty, saying, "A married woman must leave God at the altar to find Him in her domestic cares." Her ordinary food was dry bread and water, and she cared for the poor of Rome with her sister-in-law, Vannozza.

During the invasion of Rome, in 1413, Frances' husband Ponziano was captured and banished and his estates were confiscated. Soldiers destroyed their home and took their eldest son as a hostage. Frances trusted God in these losses, and blessed His holy name. When peace was restored Ponziano recovered his estates, their son returned, and Frances founded the Oblates of Mary, a group of laywomen seeking to serve the Lord. They cared for many sick during the plagues that swept Rome in the early 15th century.

Frances lived always in the presence of God, and among many visions was given constant sight of her angel guardian, who shed such a brightness around him that the Saint could read her midnight Office by this light alone. It is said that her angel lit the road with a headlight-like lantern, and thus the Church entrusts to Frances the care of drivers on the road.

Saint Frances of Rome died on the day she had foretold, March 9, 1440.

SAINT FRANCES XAVIER CABRINI

Patroness of Immigrants

Feast Day: November 13

Saint Frances Xavier Cabrini was born in Lombardi, Italy in 1850, one of 13 children. At the age of 18, she desired to become a nun, but poor health stood in her way. She helped her parents until their death, and then worked on a farm with her brothers and sisters.

One day a priest asked Frances to teach in a girls' school and she stayed for six years. At the request of her Bishop, she founded the Missionary Sisters of the Sacred Heart to care for poor children in schools and hospitals. Then, at the urging of Pope Leo XIII, she came to the United States with six nuns in 1889 to work among the Italian immigrants.

Filled with a deep trust in God and endowed with a wonderful administrative ability, this remarkable woman soon founded schools, hospitals, and orphanages in this strange land and saw them flourish in the aid of Italian immigrants and children. At the time of her death, at Chicago, Illinois, on December 22, 1917, her institute numbered houses in England, France, Spain, the United States, and South America.

In 1946, Mother Frances Xavier Cabrini became the first American citizen to be canonized when she was elevated to sainthood by Pope Pius XII.

SAINT GEMMA GALGANI

Patroness of Tuberculosis Patients

Feast Day: April 11

Gemma Galgani was born in Tuscany in 1878, the daughter of a poor pharmacist. Her mother died when she was seven years old, and from then on she continually suffered from ill health, the misunderstanding of others, and from what she believed to be the physical attacks of the devil. Through it all, however, Gemma remained at peace and enjoyed constant communion with our Lord, who spoke to her as if He were bodily present.

Gemma had a great love for the poor and helped them as much as possible. She wanted very much to be a Passionist nun, but was not accepted because of her health. In her 20's, she was miraculously cured of spinal meningitis through the intercession of Saint Gabriel Possenti. God granted Gemma visions, ecstasies, revelations, supernatural knowledge, conversation with her guardian angel, prophecy, and miracles. In 1899, she received the gift of the stigmata, and in 1903, she was diagnosed with tuberculosis. Saint Gemma Galgani died on Holy Saturday, 1903, at the age of 25 and was canonized in 1940.

O my soul, bless Jesus. Never forget the many graces He has given thee. Love that God who so loves thee. Lift thyself up to Him, who has lowered Himself for thee; show thyself as He shows Himself with thee; be clean of heart, be pure. Love thy Jesus, who has lifted thee out of so much misery. Love thy God, bless thy Lord.

– SAINT GEMMA GALGANI

SAINT GENEVIEVE

Patroness of Paris, Relief from Disasters

Feast Day: January 3

Genevieve was born at Nanterre, near Paris. At the age of seven, she made a vow of perpetual chastity with the help of Saint Germanus, who prophesied her future sanctity. Genevieve often traveled on works of mercy, which, by the gifts of prophecy and miracles, she unfailingly performed.

When Childeric, king of the Franks, besieged Paris, Genevieve went out with a few followers to procure grain for the starving citizens. Childeric, though a pagan, respected her, and at her request spared the lives of many prisoners. Later, when Attila and his Huns were approaching Paris, Genevieve directed the people not to flee, but to give themselves to prayers and penance. Suddenly Attila changed his course, and God mercifully averted the impending disaster. King Clovis, a convert from paganism, made Genevieve his constant adviser, and after a long and loving life, Saint Genevieve died in 512.

A pestilence broke out at Paris in 1129, which in a short time swept off 14,000 persons. In desperation, Parisians carried the relics of Saint Genevieve in solemn procession through the city. That same day only three persons died, the rest recovered, and the epidemic ended. This was the first of a series of miraculous favors which the city of Paris has obtained through the relics of its Patron Saint.

SAINT GIANNA BERETTA MOLLA

Patroness of Working Mothers

Feast Day: May 16

On October 4, 1922, Gianna, the tenth of 13 children, was born to Alberto and Maria Beretta in Milan, Italy. The family was deeply devout; two brothers became priests and a sister became a nun. Gianna served the poor and elderly while studying to eventually become a pediatric doctor and surgeon. An avid skier, Gianna married Pietro Molla in 1955. They had three children as she continued her medical career.

In September of 1961, Gianna was two months pregnant with their fourth child when doctors discovered a tumor in her uterus. Her surgeon recommended an abortion to save Gianna's life, but she chose only to have the tumor removed, to save the life of her unborn child. She told her husband Pietro, "If you must decide between me and the child, do not hesitate: choose the child – I insist on it. Save it."

On Holy Saturday, 1962, Gianna gave birth to Gianna Emanuela, a healthy 10 pound baby girl. Unfortunately, she developed septic peritonitis in the process, and after a week of intense suffering, during which she declined pain medication, Gianna died on April 28, at the age of 39, exclaiming, "Jesus, I love you. Jesus, I love you." Pope John Paul II canonized Saint Gianna Molla in 2004, an example of Christian motherhood in the conscious gift of herself for her children.

SAINT HEDWIG

Patroness of Brides

Feast Day: October 16

Hedwig was born in 1174, in Bavaria, Germany, the daughter of Berthold III, Duke of Croatia, and his wife Agnes. She was the aunt of Saint Elizabeth of Hungary. The Benedictine nuns of Lutzingen educated Hedwig, and at 12, she married Prince Henry the Bearded, Duke of Silesia and head of the Polish royal family.

They had seven children, and a happy home life. Hedwig and Henry lived for God, establishing convents, hospitals, and monasteries. In 1233, Henry became Duke of Greater Poland, and five years later was tragically killed in battle with the Mongols, who were attacking Eastern Europe.

Hedwig had a special zeal for the poor, whom she cared for personally, and to whom she gave much of her fortune. After Henry's death, Hedwig became a Cistercian nun at the monastery of Trebnitz. In 1241, she buried her son, Henry the Pious, who died as did his father, fighting the Mongols.

Hedwig died in the Cistercian monastery of Trebnitz on October 15, 1243. Many people reported receiving miracles after her death. Pope Clement IV canonized Saint Hedwig in 1266. She is the patron saint of Brandenburg, Berlin, as well as the patroness of Silesia, Poland. Pope John Paul II was elected Pope on her feast day, October 16, 1978.

SAINT HELEN

Patroness of Divorced People

Feast Day: August 18

Saint Helena, mother of Constantine the Great, was born in 250 AD. She married Constantius Chlorus, Co-Emperor of the Western Roman Empire, in 270. Soon after, her only son Constantine was born, and her husband divorced her to marry Theodora, stepdaughter of Co-Emperor Maximian.

After Constantius' death in 308, Constantine became emperor, and he reinstated his mother Helen as Augusta, or Empress. Helen converted to Christianity in 312, after Constantine's fateful victory over Maxentius at the Milvian Bridge, which he attributed to "the God of the Christians," since the Lord had commanded him to place the sign of the cross on his soldiers' battle standards. In 313, Constantine ended the persecution of Christians with his famous Edict of Milan.

Empress Helen used her position and wealth to help the poor, build churches, and spread Christianity throughout the empire, including the Holy Land, which she visited at the age of 80, where she discovered the True Cross of Christ.

Saint Helen died in 330, with her son Constantine by her side.

SAINT HILDA

Patroness of the Arts

Feast Day: November 17

The English princess Hilda was born in 614 in Suffolk, England, and was baptized by Saint Paulinus in 627. At 33, Hilda entered Chelles Monastery in France, but returned to England at Saint Aidan's request to become abbess of the double monastery of Hartlepool and later, of Whitby, where monks and nuns lived separately in adjoining convents. She followed the rule of Saint Columbanus in her convents. During her tenure at Whitby, five of the monks became bishops, giving great service to the Anglo-Saxon Church in its struggle with paganism.

Hilda loved the study of God's Word in Holy Scripture, and helped many people convert to Jesus and the Catholic faith. Because of her virtue, the great and humble alike came to seek her counsel. She was patroness of the arts and helped her friend, Saint Caedmon, the great poet, in his faith journey as well. During the last seven years of her life, Hilda suffered from a continuous high fever and lingering illness; even so, she continued to thank and praise God for everything and neglected none of her duties to God and her people.

Saint Hilda, considered one of England's greatest women, died on November 17, 680, and the tolling of a monastery bell was heard miraculously miles away, where a devout nun saw angels carrying Saint Hilda's soul to heaven.

SAINT JANE FRANCES DE CHANTAL

Patroness of Widows

Feast Day: December 12; August 18 (USA)

Jane Frances de Fremiot was born in Burgundy, France, in 1572. A short time later, her mother died, and she was placed under the care of a worldly-minded governess. In this crisis she offered herself to the Mother of God, and secured Mary's protection for life. At 20, she married the Baron de Chantal, and as a loving and beloved wife and mother of four, she made her house the pattern of a Christian home.

At 28, Jane's husband was shot in a hunting accident, and died in her arms. Her sorrow as a widow was increased by friends who urged her to marry again. She branded on her heart the name of Jesus, and decided to live for God alone.

In 1604, Jane met Saint Francis de Sales, and in 1610 she established with him the Visitation Order, for women who had been rejected by other orders due to age or health reasons. The Visitation Nuns lived a contemplative life and served widows and women in poor health.

Jane endured interior desolation, sickness, opposition, the death of family members, and even the death of Saint Francis himself, while establishing 87 houses of her Order. In 1641, at the age of 70, Jane died.

Saint Jane Frances de Chantal was canonized in 1767, and is the patroness of widows, forgotten people and parents separated from their children.

SAINT JEANNE DE LESTONNAC

Patroness of Abuse Victims

Feast Day: February 2

Jeanne de Lestonnac was born into French aristocracy on May 5, 1555, the daughter of a Catholic father and a Calvinist mother, which made for a childhood of misery and abuse. Jeanne was a sensitive, affectionate child who chose her father's faith as her own, thereby earning the extreme dislike of her mother. In her sorrow, Jeanne turned to Mary, our heavenly mother, for consolation and guidance, and received from Our Lady compassion for others who were mistreated.

Jeanne fell in love with and married Gaston de Montferrand. They had seven children, two of whom entered religious life. Her husband died when Jeanne was 41, leaving her to run her estate and castle alone. At 46, Jeanne entered the Cistercian monastery at Toulouse, France. However, the rigorous Cistercian life was too much for her, and she became seriously ill. Jeanne asked to die at the convent, but her superiors chose for her to leave the convent and return to the world.

In disappointment, Jeanne cried out to God. Suddenly she had the answer: "Begin a new community to help educate young women." In 1606 she founded the Sisters of the Company of Mary, devoted to education and combating the errors of Calvinism. Pope Paul V approved the congregation, and as superior, Jeanne oversaw her young order's growth. Saint Jeanne de Lestonnac died on February 2, 1640, at the age of 85, and was canonized in 1949.

SAINT JOAN OF ARC

Patroness of Servicewomen

Feast Day: May 30

On January 6, 1412, Joan of Arc was born in Domremy, France. At a very early age, she heard the voices of saints, whose messages at first were personal and general. Then, in May, 1428, her voices "of Saint Michael, Saint Catherine, and Saint Margaret," told Joan to go to King Charles VII of France and help him reconquer his kingdom. At that time the English king was after the throne of France, and the Duke of Burgundy sided with him to gobble up ever more French territory.

After overcoming opposition from churchmen and courtiers, 17-year-old Joan wondrously ended the siege of Orleans with a small army on May 8, 1429. She then enjoyed a series of spectacular military successes, during which King Charles was able to enter Rheims and be crowned with her at his side.

In May 1430, as Joan was attempting to relieve the city of Compiegne, she was captured by the Burgundians and sold to the English when King Charles and the French did nothing to save her. After months of imprisonment, she was tried by a tribunal presided over by the infamous Bishop Peter Cauchon, who hoped the English would help him to become archbishop.

Through her unfamiliarity with the technicalities of theology, Joan was trapped into making a few damaging statements. When she refused to retract the assertion that it was the saints of God who had commanded her to do what she had done, Joan was condemned to death as a heretic and burned at the stake on May 30, 1431, at the age of 19. In 1456, another Catholic tribunal exonerated Joan of all guilt. Pope Benedict XV canonized Saint Joan of Arc in 1920, making official what the faithful had known for centuries.

SAINT JOSEPHINE BAKHITA

Patroness of Sudan

Feast Day: February 8

Josephine Bakhita was born to a wealthy family at Darfur, Sudan in 1868. Slave-traders kidnapped her at the tender age of 9 and gave her the name Bakhita – the fortunate one. They sold and resold this frightened, afflicted girl, until finally Callisto Legnani, the Italian consul, purchased her in 1883. Legnani had planned to free Bakhita, but gave her to his friend Augusto Michielli as nanny for his baby daughter Mimmina.

During Mimmina's baptismal preparation by the Canossian Sisters, Bakhita learned of the Catholic Church and was baptized in 1890, taking the name Josephine. When the Michiellis tried to take her back to Africa with them, Josephine refused. In court, the judge ruled that since slavery was illegal in Italy, she had actually been free since 1885.

In 1896, Josephine consecrated herself forever to God as a nun in the Order of Saint Magdalene of Canossa. In 1902, she was transferred to Schio, where she remained until her death in 1947, serving as door-keeper, cook, seamstress, and in other ministries of love for her fellow sisters and community. She would lay her hands on the heads of the little school children who would run to the door, and speak to them in her musical, rhythmical voice, encouraging all who came to her.

Saint Josephine Bakhita, the first saint from the Sudan, was canonized in 2000 by Pope John Paul II. She now enjoys eternal joy with the One Master of us all.

SAINT JULIA

Patroness of Suffering Victims

Feast Day: May 23

Julia was a noble virgin of Carthage in North Africa, who, when the city was taken by the Vandal King Genseric in 439, was sold for a slave to a pagan Syrian merchant named Eusebius. By cheerfulness and patience, Julia found happiness and comfort in the middle of her difficulties. She devoted herself to prayer and reading books of piety whenever she wasn't busy serving her master. Eusebius, who was charmed with her fidelity and other virtues, took Julia with him on one of his voyages to Gaul. Having reached the northern part of Corsica, he went onshore to join the pagans of the place in an idolatrous festival.

Julia was left some distance away because she refused to join in the superstitious ceremonies. Felix, the governor of the island, asked who this woman was who dared to insult the gods. Eusebius informed him that she was a Christian, and that all his authority over her was too weak to force her to renounce her religion, but that he found her so diligent and faithful he could not part with her.

While Eusebius was drunk and asleep, Governor Felix tried to force Julia to sacrifice to his gods. He offered to free her if she would comply. Julia answered that she was as free as she desired to be as long as she was allowed to serve Jesus Christ. Felix struck her on the face and had his soldiers tear out her hair and crucify her. Saint Julia remained loyal to her True Master, in life and in death.

SAINT JULIANA FALCONIERI

Patroness of the Chronically Ill

Feast Day: June 19

Juliana Falconieri was born in 1270 in answer to prayer. Her father built the beautiful church of the Annunziata in Florence, while her uncle, Blessed Alexis, was one of the founders of the Servite Order. Under his care Juliana grew up, "more like an angel than a human being." It is said that she never used a mirror or gazed upon the face of a man during her whole life. The mere mention of sin made her shudder and tremble. Her devotion to Our Lady drew her to the Servants of Mary, and at 14 she received the habit from Saint Philip Benizi himself.

Julia's holiness attracted many novices, and she reluctantly became foundress of the Servite Order of Mary. She served her sisters as their servant rather than their superior, while outside her convent she led a life of apostolic charity, converting sinners, reconciling enemies, and healing the sick. She would sometimes go into ecstasy for whole days, and her prayers saved the Servite Order when it was in danger of being suppressed.

Saint Julia suffered from a serious stomach disease which kept her from eating. She bore her agony cheerfully, grieving only for the deprivation of Holy Communion. On her deathbed she begged to once more to see and adore the Blessed Sacrament. A priest reverently laid the Host on a corporal, which was placed over her heart. When she took her last breath, the Host disappeared, and the image of the cross stamped on the Host was found on her breast. Saint Juliana died on June 12, 1340.

SAINT JUSTINA

Patroness of Spiritual Warfare

Feast Day: September 26

The superstition of Saint Cyprian's idolatrous parents devoted him from his infancy to the devil, and he was brought up in all the dark mysteries of idolatry, astrology, and sorcery. When Cyprian had learned all these errors and delusions, he blasphemed Christ, and committed secret crimes and murders.

There lived at Antioch a young Christian lady called Justina, of high birth and great beauty. A pagan nobleman fell deeply in love with her, and when she would not give in to his advances, he applied to Cyprian for assistance. Cyprian, no less smitten for the lady, tried every secret with which he was acquainted to conquer her resolution. Justina, perceiving herself vigorously attacked, armed herself by prayer, watchfulness, and mortification against all his tricks and the power of his spells. Finding himself powerless over her, Cyprian resolved to leave sorcery and become a Christian.

Cyprian and Justina were seized and presented to the same judge. She was inhumanly scourged, and Cyprian was torn with iron hooks. After this they were both sent in chains to Diocletian, who commanded their heads to be struck off, and Saint Cyprian and Saint Justina entered heaven together!

Let us beg of God to send us grace to resist temptation, and to do His holy will in all things.

SAINT KATERI TEKAKWITHA

Lily of the Mohawks

Co-Patroness of Environment and Ecology

Feast Day: July 14

Tekakwitha – *She who bumps into things* – was born near Auriesville, New York in 1656. Her father, a Mohawk warrior and her mother, a Christian Algonquin, both died along with her infant brother in a smallpox epidemic that left Tekakwitha with weakened eyesight and her face scarred for life.

Tekakwitha was living with her uncle and aunt when the Jesuit "Blackrobes" came to her village. Although her family disapproved, she told the priests she wanted to be a Christian, and on Easter Sunday, 1676, Kateri (Catherine) Tekakwitha was baptized into the Body of Christ.

Kateri greatly loved Our Lord and His Mother Mary. Even so, her family insulted her, treated her poorly, and tried to have her marry against her will. Kateri escaped over a long arduous route of over 300 miles to Sault Sainte Marie, Canada, where she found refuge at the Saint Francis Xavier Mission. She received her first Holy Communion there on Christmas Day, 1677, as her poor eyes shone with the light of Jesus.

Kateri kindly cared for children, the sick, and the elderly. She spent long hours in prayer and penance, consecrating herself to Jesus in 1679. After a long bout with illness, Kateri died on April 17, 1680. Pope John Paul II beatified Kateri, and on October 21, 2012, Pope Benedict XVI canonized Kateri Tekakwitha, the first Native American to be declared a Saint!

SAINT KATHARINE DREXEL

Patroness of Heart Ailments

Feast Day: March 3

Saint Katharine Drexel was born in 1858, into a prominent Philadelphia family. Katharine became imbued with love for God and neighbor. She took an avid interest in the material and spiritual well-being of Black and Native Americans. She began by donating money but soon concluded that more was needed – the lacking ingredient was people.

In 1891, Katharine founded the Sisters of the Blessed Sacrament for Indians and Colored People, known today as the Sisters of the Blessed Sacrament, whose members would work for the betterment of those they were called to serve. From the age of 33 until her death in 1955, she dedicated her life and a fortune of 20 million dollars to this work.

In 1894, Mother Drexel took part in opening the first mission school for Indians, in Santa Fe, New Mexico. Dozens of schools quickly followed: for Native Americans west of the Mississippi River, and for the Blacks in the southern part of the United States as well. In 1915 Mother Drexel founded Xavier University in New Orleans. At her death there were more than 500 Sisters teaching in 63 schools throughout the country.

Saint Katharine Drexel was canonized by Pope John Paul II on October 1, 2000.

SAINT LILLIAN

Patroness of Brave Martyrs

Feast Day: July 27

Lillian, also known as Liliosa, was a married woman who lived in 9th century Andalusia, an area of southern Spain that was controlled by the Muslims from 711 to 1236.

In the city of Córdoba, between 850 and 860 AD, Islamic rulers executed 48 Christians, mostly priests, for religious offenses, in particular, declaring emphatically the divinity of Jesus. Lillian and her husband Saint Felix were two of these.

Lillian had lived her Christian faith secretly, so as not to arouse the suspicions of her Muslim neighbors. Felix's relative Aurelius and his wife Sabigotho were also secret Christians.

One day Aurelius witnessed the scourging of a Christian merchant, and the two couples decided it was time to publicly witness to their faith, regardless of the consequences. They began visiting Christians imprisoned in the jails of Córdoba, where they met a priest named Eulogius, who kept records on the martyrs and wrote about them in order to encourage other believers to be strong in their faith.

On July 23, 852, the four friends, together with Father George, a Palestinian Christian, entered church, the women with their faces unveiled. The guards arrested them and brought them all before the magistrate. They continued to profess their Christianity, and, four days later, the five were martyred.

Saint Lillian, courageous Christian, pray for us.

SAINT LOUISE DE MARILLAC

Patroness of Social Workers

Feast Day: March 15

Louise de Marillac was born in 1591 at Meux, France. She lost her parents by age 15. Her ill health kept her from the convent, and she married in 1611. Her husband died four years later, and Louise came under the direction of Saint Vincent de Paul.

Saint Vincent realized that Louise, although feeble, was smart, humble, and physically strong. He sent her on missions to the poor and sick, and soon four young women joined her to continue the ministry. Under Saint Vincent's guidance, Louise drew up the rule for the Sisters of Charity, and together they founded the Order in 1642. Saint Vincent told the nuns, "Your convent will be the house of the sick; your cell, a hired room; your chapel, the parish church; your cloister, the streets of the city or the wards of the hospital."

The new community sought to aid the numerous neglected children on the streets. Louise traveled throughout France, establishing her Order in hospitals, orphanages, and elsewhere. By the time of her death in 1660, Saint Louise de Marillac had founded over 40 houses in France. In 1960, Pope John XXIII declared Saint Louise the patron of social workers. Her incorrupt body today lies in the chapel of the Daughters of Charity in Paris.

SAINT LUCY

Patroness of Eye Afflictions

Feast Day: December 13

The mother of Saint Lucy suffered four years from an issue of blood, and no one was able to help her. Saint Lucy reminded her mother that a woman in the Gospel had been healed of the same disorder. "Saint Agatha," she said, "stands ever in the sight of Him for Whom she died. Only touch her tomb with faith, and you will be healed."

Mother and daughter spent the night praying by the tomb, until, overcome by weariness, both fell asleep. Saint Agatha appeared in a vision to Saint Lucy, calling her sister, and foretold her mother's recovery and her own martyrdom. Lucy's mother was instantly healed, and in her gratitude she allowed Lucy to distribute her wealth among the poor, and consecrate her virginity to Christ.

A young man to whom Lucy had been promised in marriage accused her as a Christian to the authorities, but Our Lord, by a special miracle, saved from outrage this virgin whom He had chosen for His own. The fire kindled around her did her no harm. Then the sword was plunged into her heart, and the promise made at the tomb of Saint Agatha was fulfilled.

SAINT MADELEINE SOPHIE BARAT

Patroness of Humble Superiors

Feast Day: May 25

Madeleine Sophie Barat was born in France in 1779, as her country was just recovering from the ravages of the Revolution. Her seminarian brother Louis homeschooled her, and brought her to Paris at 16 for her continued education, where she came under the direction of Father Joseph Varin. Under his direction Madeleine and a few companions founded the Society of the Sacred Heart in 1801, devoted to the Sacred Heart and dedicated to the education of girls.

In the course of her 63 years as Superior General of the Society, Madeleine built 105 houses of the Order in the principal countries of the world. When authorities closed convents in France in the aftermath of the French Revolution, Madeleine opened up new ones in other countries, including the United States. She exhorted her Religious at all times to seek the glory of the Heart of Jesus in laboring for the sanctification of souls. "Those who see one of ours, ought to be able to say: 'That is a Religious of the Sacred Heart; we know her by her meekness and humility.'"

Madeleine's unfailing serenity and sweetness cheered and encouraged all who came in contact with her. "To suffer myself and not to make others suffer," was one of her favorite mottoes.

Saint Madeleine Sophie Barat died at Paris on Ascension Thursday, 1865, and was canonized May 24, 1925.

SAINT MARCELLA

Patroness of Holy Women

Feast Day: January 31

Saint Marcella, whom Saint Jerome called the glory of the Roman women, became a widow in the seventh month after her marriage. Having determined to consecrate the remainder of her days to the service of God, she rejected the hand of Cerealis, the consul, uncle of Gallus Caesar, and resolved to imitate the lives of the ascetics of the East. She abstained from wine and spent all her time in spiritual reading, prayer, and visiting the shrines of the martyrs.

Other women followed Marcella's example, and met with her in her mansion on the Aventine Hill. They put themselves under the direction of Saint Jerome, and Rome was in a short time filled with monasteries. When the Goths under Alaric plundered Rome in 410, they captured and scourged Marcella severely, in order to make her surrender the treasures which she had long before given to the poor. She cared only for the innocence of her dear spiritual daughter, Principia, and begged the soldiers with many tears to not harm her.

Moved with compassion, the soldiers released Marcella and Principia, and brought them to the Church of Saint Paul, to which Alaric had granted the right of sanctuary. Shortly thereafter, Saint Marcella closed her eyes by a happy death, in the arms of Saint Principia, near the end of August, 410.

SAINT MARGARET OF ANTIOCH

Patroness of Expectant Mothers

Feast Day: July 20

Margaret of Antioch was born late in the 3rd century, and lived in the area of modern-day Turkey. Her father was a pagan priest, and her mother died soon after Margaret's birth. Theotimus, her Christian nurse, taught Margaret about Jesus, and she became a Christian and consecrated her virginity to God. When Margaret's father learned of this, he disowned his daughter and threw her out of the house.

Theotimus adopted Margaret, who tended sheep for her. One day, a Roman prefect named Olybrius noticed Margaret in the field and sought to marry her. When she refused his advances because of her vow, he brought her to trial and commanded her to renounce her faith in Christ. However, Margaret chose Jesus, and Olybrius had her tortured and imprisoned.

The soldiers tried to burn Margaret, but the flames would not touch her. They then tried to drown her in a huge cauldron of boiling water, but as she prayed, her chains fell off, and she emerged unhurt, causing the conversion of many witnesses.

Back in prison, Satan appeared as a terrible dragon that tried to swallow her. Margaret made the sign of the cross and the cross she carried enlarged until it split open his stomach! Finally, the Emperor Diocletian beheaded her.

Saint Margaret became a very popular saint across Europe, especially in England, and is invoked for help in childbirth.

SAINT MARGARET MARY ALACOQUE

Patroness of the Sacred Heart

Feast Day: October 17

Saint Margaret Mary was born on July 22 in Burgundy, France, and sent to the Poor Clares' school at Charolles on the death of her father, when she was eight years old. Bedridden for five years with rheumatic fever, Margaret early developed a devotion to the Blessed Sacrament. In 1671 she entered the Visitation convent at Paray-le-Monial.

In a series of visions over 18 months, Jesus revealed to Sister Margaret Mary that she was His chosen instrument to spread devotion to His Sacred Heart, instructed her in a devotion now known as the Nine First Fridays and the Holy Hour, and asked that the feast of the Sacred Heart be established. Rebuffed by her superior in her efforts to carry out her mission, Margaret Mary eventually won her over but was unable to convince either theologians or her fellow sisters of the validity of her apparitions.

Thankfully, Margaret did receive the support of Saint Claude de La Colombiere, the community's confessor, who declared that her visions were genuine. In 1683, opposition in the community ended when Margaret Mary was named Assistant to the Superior. Within a short time, the community built a chapel to honor the Sacred Heart, and devotion to the Sacred Heart spread rapidly to other Visitation convents.

Saint Margaret Mary died at Paray-le-Monial in 1690, and was canonized in 1920. She, Saint John Eudes, and Saint Claude de La Colombiere are called the "Saints of the Sacred Heart." The devotion was officially recognized and approved by Pope Clement XIII in 1765.

SAINT MARGARET OF SCOTLAND

Patroness of Large Families

Feast Day: November 16

Born in Hungary in 1045, Margaret, whose name means *pearl*, spent her youth in England as an English princess before fleeing the invading William the Conqueror in 1066. King Malcolm of Scotland assisted Margaret and her mother, who had shipwrecked off the Scottish coast, and he married Margaret in 1070.

As Queen, Margaret's quiet and holy disposition helped to transform both King and court. Together she and King Malcolm personally fed the poor and brought justice to their country. Margaret zealously built churches and monasteries, making vestments herself; she could not rest till she saw the laws of God and His Church observed throughout her realm.

Margaret took good care of her home and eight children, rising in the night with her husband to pray and seek God. Their sanctity was the fruit of her prudence and zeal.

On her deathbed Margaret received the news that her husband and her eldest son were slain in battle. She replied, "I thank You, Almighty God, for sending me so great a sorrow to purify me from my sins."

Saint Margaret died at Edinburgh Castle, Scotland, on November 16, 1093. She had indeed found the pearl of great price, and had given all she had to gain Him.

SAINT MARIA GORETTI

Patroness of Youth

Feast Day: July 6

Born in Italy on October 16, 1890, Maria Goretti was a happy and obedient child. When she was nine years old, her farmworker father died. Maria prayed each day for the strength to follow Jesus and avoid serious sin.

One day a young neighbor named Alexander tried to rape Maria when he found her alone in the farmhouse. She refused, saying, "I would rather die than sin." In a rage, Alexander stabbed Maria fourteen times with a long knife. Twelve-year-old Maria lived only twenty-four hours; but before dying she forgave Alexander and prayed for his conversion.

Alexander was sentenced to 30 years in prison. While there one night he saw a vision of Maria, dressed in white, gathering lilies in a garden. She smiled at him and offered him an armful of lilies. As he took them, each lily changed into a still white flame. Then Maria disappeared. Alexander called for a priest, repented of his sins, and surrendered his life to Jesus. After his release, Alexander asked forgiveness of Maria's mother and family, and spent his life serving God.

Alexander and many of Maria's family were in Rome in 1950, when Pope Pius XII canonized the new patroness for Catholic youth: Saint Maria Goretti!

BLESSED MARIE-ROSE DUROCHER

Patroness of the Seriously Ill

Feast Day: October 6

Eulalia Durocher was born October 6, 1811, near Montreal, Canada, the tenth of eleven children. Because of her poor health, she could not enter religious life. When Eulalia was 18, her mother died, and she went with her father to live with and keep house for her brother, Father Theophile. Eulalia grew close to Jesus and Mary as she unselfishly served her family.

19th-century Canada was a wild and wooly place, and its shepherd, Bishop Ignace Bourget, searched Europe for priests and nuns to help care for his flock. Eulalia also saw the great need to instruct the young, especially girls. In 1843, Bishop Bourget invited Eulalia to found a new community of women dedicated to education. At the age of 32, with two friends in a little home in Longuieul, across the Saint Lawrence River, Eulalia founded the Sisters of the Holy Names of Jesus and Mary and took the name Marie Rose.

As superior of the young order, Mother Marie Rose wisely and carefully guided the new congregation through great poverty and other challenges as they taught the young of the far-flung Canadian society. Most of all, she remained totally dedicated to serving the poor.

After a six-year illness, Mother Marie Rose died at the young age of 38. Pope John Paul II declared her Blessed Marie Rose Durocher on May 23, 1982.

SAINT MARTHA

Patroness of Homemakers

Feast Day: July 29

Saint John tells us that Jesus loved Martha and Mary and Lazarus, and yet but few glimpses are shown of them. First, the sisters are set before us with a word. Martha received Jesus into her house, and was busy in outward, loving, lavish service, while Mary sat in silence at the feet she had bathed with her tears. Then, their brother is ill, and they send to Jesus, "Lord, he whom You love is sick." And in His own time the Lord came, and they go out to meet Him; and then follows that scene of unutterable tenderness and of sublimity unsurpassed: the silent waiting of Mary; Martha strong in faith, but realizing so vividly, with her practical turn of mind, the fact of death, and hesitating: "Can You show Your wonders in the grave?"

Once again, on the eve of His Passion, we see Jesus at Bethany. Martha, true to her character, is serving: Mary, as at first, pours the precious ointment, in adoration and love, on His divine head.

When the storm of persecution came, the family of Bethany, with a few companions, was put into a boat, without oars or sail, and borne to the coast of France. Saint Mary's tomb is at Saint Baume, Saint Lazarus is venerated as the founder of the Church of Marseilles, and the memory of the virtues and labors of Saint Martha is still fragrant at Avignon and Tarascon.

SAINT MARY OF EGYPT

Patroness of Reformed Prostitutes

Feast Day: April 3

Mary of Egypt was a beautiful, spoiled, rich girl who at the age of 12 left her father's house that she might sin without restraint, and for 17 years she lived in shame at Alexandria. Then she accompanied a pilgrimage to Jerusalem, hoping to lure others into sin. On the Feast of the Exaltation of the Holy Cross, Mary went with the crowd to the church which contained the precious wood. The rest entered and adored; but Mary was invisibly held back. In that instant her misery and exclusion burst upon her, and she was filled with remorse.

Mary repented of her sin, and turning to a statue of Our Lady, she vowed from then on to do penance if she might enter and stand like Mary Magdalen beside the Cross. Then she entered in. As she knelt before Our Lady on leaving the church, she heard a voice saying, "Pass over Jordan, and you will find rest."

Saint Mary went into the wilderness across the Jordan River, and lived as a hermit nearly 50 years. In 420, she met the Abbot Zosimus. She told him that for 17 years the old songs and scenes had haunted her; after that, she knew perfect peace. At her request, he brought her Holy Communion on Holy Thursday. She asked him to return again after a year, and this time he found only her corpse upon the sand, with an inscription saying, "Bury here the body of Mary the sinner."

SAINT MARY MAGDALEN

Patroness of Converts

Feast Day: July 22

Mary was from the town of Magdala, in northern Galilee. Tradition tells us that she was a sinner, a woman from whom Christ had expelled seven demons (SEE LUKE 8:2). From the depth of her degradation she raised her eyes to Jesus with sorrow, hope, and love. All covered with shame, she came in where Jesus was at prayer, and knelt behind him. She said not a word, but bathed His feet with her tears, wiped them with the hair of her head, kissed them in humility, and at their touch her sins and her stain were gone. Then she poured on them the costly oils, and Jesus removed her reproach, gave her absolution, and told her to go in peace. From then on, Mary Magdalen ministered to Jesus, sat at His feet, and heard His words.

Mary Magdalen stood courageously with Mother Mary and Saint John at the foot of the cross, when the others had fled. On the morning of the Resurrection, Jesus appeared to her, calling her by name. He told her "But go to my brothers and tell them, 'I am going to my Father and your Father, to my God and your God.'" (JOHN 20:17) Filled with joy, Mary ran to the apostles, crying, "I have seen the Lord!"

SAINT MARY MAGDALENE DE PAZZI

Patroness of Hope in Sickness

Feast Day: May 25

Catherine de Pazzi was born in 1566 in Florence, Italy, the only daughter of Camille and Maria de Pazzi. As a child she loved to go off by herself and enter into prayer with God, who revealed Himself to her as her Creator, Redeemer, and Sanctifier. One day Catherine made a crown of thorns, and wore it for an entire night, enduring great pain. She later took a vow of virginity and taught poor children about Jesus.

Catherine entered the Carmelites at the age of 16, changing her name to Sister Mary Magdalene. She took as her motto, "Either suffer or die." Sister Magdalene's life thereafter was one of penance for sins not her own, and of love for Our Lord. She was obedient, observant of the Rule, humble and mortified, and had a great reverence for the religious life. One day, when she seemed to be at the last hour of her life, she rose from her sickbed and hastened everywhere throughout the convent, saying during her ecstasy, "O Love! O Love! No one knows You, no one knows You, no one loves You!"

Mary Magdalene de Pazzi prayed fervently for the Church and asked her Sisters to love only Our Lord Jesus Christ, to place all their hope in Him, and to be perpetually ardent with the desire to suffer for love of Him.

Saint Mary Magdalene de Pazzi died in 1607. Her body remains incorrupt to this day at her monastery in Florence.

SAINT MATILDA

Patroness of Large Families

Feast Day: March 14

Matilda was born in 895, the daughter of Count Dietrich and Countess Reinhild of Germany. Her grandmother, the Abbess of Eufurt convent, raised Matilda until her marriage in 909 to King Henry of Saxony, who became king of all Germany in 919. They enjoyed 23 years of marriage together before Henry died suddenly in 936.

Queen Matilda supported her son Henry's claim to the throne, but his brother Otto was elected instead. Henry revolted a number of times before his death in 955. Matilda founded several Benedictine monasteries and convents in the following years, and ruled the country when her son Otto went to Rome in 962, where he was crowned King Otto the Great of the Holy Roman Empire.

The people of Germany loved Matilda for her generosity to the poor and love of the sick and imprisoned. Her son Saint Bruno became the Archbishop of Cologne, her daughter Gerberga married King Louis IV of France, and her daughter Hedwig became the mother of Hugh Capet, founder of the Capetian dynasty.

Saint Matilda died at the monastery of Quedlinburg, Germany, on March 14th, 968, and was buried beside her husband.

SAINT MELANIA

Patroness of Parents Who Have Lost Children

Feast Day: December 31

Melania was born in 383 to two wealthy Christian parents, the Roman Senator Publicola and his wife Albina, who arranged a marriage for Melania to Valerius Pinianus at 14. After the unfortunate death of their two young children, and to flee the invading Visogoths, Valerius and Melania fled Rome to North Africa in 410, where they met Saint Augustine of Hippo. They built two monasteries for him, and supported the Church.

Valerius and Melania agreed to live as brother and sister, took vows of celibacy, freed their slaves, sold their lands, and gave their money to the poor, aiding churches and monasteries in Europe. In 417 Melania's mother accompanied them to Jerusalem, where Melania came to know Saint Jerome and also Saint Paulinus of Nola.

Melania gave money to monasteries in Egypt, Syria, and Palestine. After her mother and husband died in 431 and 432, Melania attracted followers and built a convent on the Mount of Olives, of which she was Abbess until her death on December 31, 439.

A good name is more desirable than great riches,
and high esteem, than gold and silver.

–PROVERBS 22:1

SAINT MONICA

Patroness of Abuse Victims

Feast Day: August 27

Monica, the mother of Saint Augustine, was born in 333. After a girlhood of singular innocence and piety, she was given in marriage to Patricius, a pagan. She at once devoted herself to his conversion, praying for him always, and winning his reverence and love by the holiness of her life and her affectionate forbearance. She was rewarded by seeing her husband baptized a year before his death.

The great hardship of her life was the conduct of her son, Augustine, who was 17 years of age when his father died in 371. His mother prayed fervently for his conversion. When Augustine left Monica in Africa to go to Italy, she followed him and found him at Milan, where the words of Saint Ambrose had already convinced him of the falsehood of Manichaean doctrines, which he abandoned without being entirely converted.

In August, 386, Saint Monica had the long-coveted happiness of seeing her son return to God. Augustine was baptized by Saint Ambrose on Easter Sunday the following year and soon after, with his mother and some friends, he set out for Africa. But Saint Monica's work was done; her son was converted; the sinner had become a saint. She fell sick on the road and died at Ostia in 387.

Son, nothing in this world now affords me delight. I do not know what there is now for me to do or why I am still here, all my hopes in this world being now fulfilled.

—Saint Monica, after the conversion of her son, Augustine

SAINT NATALIA

Patroness of Loyal Wives

Feast Day: December 1

Natalia was a 3rd century Christian married to Adrian, a pagan imperial officer. While presiding over the torture of a group of Christians, he asked them what reward they expected from God for their sacrifice. They replied, quoting Saint Paul's letter to the Corinthians, "Eye has not seen, nor has ear heard, neither has it entered the heart of man, the things God has prepared for those who love him."

Adrian was so amazed at their courage that he publically confessed, "Let me be counted as one of these, for I too am a Christian!" When Natalia learned of his declaration and subsequent arrest, she arranged for Adrian to be taught the faith in prison.

Adrian was sentenced to death, and all visitors were forbidden. Even so, Natalia disguised herself as boy and bribed her way in to see him and ask his prayers for her in heaven. She then accompanied her husband to his execution. As the executioner cut off Adrian's limbs, one at a time, she prayed for him and encouraged him. She also took one of his dismembered hands.

Adrian's body and those of the other martyrs were burned at a huge fire, but a rainstorm came up which extinguished the flames, and the Christians buried their remains. Later, Natalia sailed to Argyropolis, near Constantinople, where she died in 311.

SAINT PAULA

Patroness of Widows

Feast Day: January 26

Paula was born in Rome of noble parents on May 5, 347. She married Senator Toxotius, and they had five children: Toxotius, Saint Blesilla, Pauline, Saint Eustochium, and Rufina.

When Toxotius died an early death in 379, the 32-year-old Paula renounced the world and devoted herself to serving the poor. Paula was a friend and sister in the Lord to Saints Marcella, Epiphanius, and Paulinus of Antioch. Through their influence, Paula became a model for Christian widows.

In 382, Paula met Saint Jerome when he came to Rome. Under his tutelage, she and her daughter Eustochium learned Hebrew to study the Scripture. In 384, Paula's daughter Blesilla died, leaving her heartbroken. Paula left Rome the next year with Eustochium and journeyed to the Holy Land, where she settled in Bethlehem under the spiritual direction of Saint Jerome. She and her daughter build a hospice, monastery, and convent, which Paula headed as abbess.

Paula became Saint Jerome's closest friend and helper, taking care of him and helping him in his renowned biblical masterwork. She also built numerous churches, at great financial cost to herself.

Saint Paula died in Bethlehem on January 26, 404. Saint Jerome wrote her biography, and Saint Paula is buried under the Church of the Nativity in Bethlehem.

SAINTS PERPETUA AND FELICITY

Patronesses of Martyrs

Feast Day: March 7

Perpetua was a noble laywoman born to a Christian mother and pagan father. In 203 she accepted Christ and was baptized, during the persecutions of Emperor Septimus. Perpetua's father tried to discourage her, but pointing to a water jug she asked him if he could call it by any other name than what it was. "Of course not," he replied. Perpetua retorted, "Neither can I call myself by any other name than what I am – a Christian."

Perpetua had a baby son whom she was still nursing when she was arrested and imprisoned for the Faith. The soldiers also imprisoned two Christian slaves, Felicity and Revocatus, as well as the believers Saturninus and Secundulus. The Lord told Perpetua to pray for endurance in the face of her trials.

Perpetua left a record of her imprisonment called *The Martyrdom of Perpetua and Felicity*, which became so popular that it was read during Mass in the early centuries. She relates that the dark prison was crowded with prisoners, the heat was suffocating, and she was very much afraid. Thankfully, Perpetua was relocated to a better cell and allowed to nurse her baby. "My prison became my palace."

Felicity gave birth in prison to a healthy girl who was raised by a Christian woman. Perpetua, Felicity, and their companions were martyred by the sword on March 7, in Carthage, North Africa, faithful to Christ to the end.

SAINT PHILOMENA

Patroness of Babies, Children of Mary

Feast Day: August 11 (non-liturgical)

In 1802 the remains of a young woman were discovered in the catacomb of Saint Priscilla in Rome, along with a small glass vial of her blood and drawings of anchors, arrows, and a palm. The arranged tiles covering her body proclaimed: *Pax Tecum Filumena* – Peace be with you, Philomena. These signs indicated she was a virgin and martyr, unknown until then.

In 1805 a priest passing the relics of Saint Philomena suddenly felt a strong spiritual joy and he requested permission to enshrine the relics at a chapel in Mugnano, Italy. Pilgrims at the shrine began reporting cures of cancer and other healings, including the healing of Venerable Pauline Jaricot, who reported being cured of a severe heart condition overnight – the Miracle of Mugnano.

Saint Philomena became the only person recognized as a saint solely on the basis of miraculous intercession. She has, however, been the object of great devotion of many saints, notably Saint John Vianney. Many wonderful favors have been obtained through her intercession. Beginning with Pope Leo, a number of popes have authorized her public veneration.

In private revelation to Mother Luisa di Gesu and Fr. Di Lucia, Saint Philomena disclosed that she was a virgin who was tortured and martyred at the age of 14 in the third century, choosing Christ over the advances of the Roman Emperor.

SAINT PRISCILLA

Patroness of the Roman Martyrs

Feast Day: January 16

Saint Priscilla was the widow of the Roman Consul Mancius Aeilius Glabrio. Tradition has it that Saint Peter arrived in Rome around 40 AD, and stayed at their home, located on the Via Salaria, using it as his headquarters in Rome. Priscilla and Mancius were the parents of Saint Pudens, a Roman Senator, and the grandparents of Pudentiana and her three brothers, all of whom are saints. Saint Pudens' home, sometimes called the church of Saint Pudentiana, is said to be the first place where Saint Peter celebrated Mass in Rome.

Priscilla's husband Mancius was executed by the Emperor Domitian, most probably because he was a Christian. Priscilla herself was also martyred in Rome. Although her dates are unknown, the name Priscilla, or Prisca, is mentioned often by early writers of Roman Church history. The Catacomb of Saint Priscilla located under her home bears her name.

Romans often built underground areas under their homes, in the soft tufa stone upon which Rome is built. Because early Christians disapproved of cremation, they chose to bury their dead, especially the martyrs, in underground vaults outside the city known as catacombs. The Christians would pray and celebrate Mass in the catacombs as well. After Constantine ended the persecutions, the Christians moved the bodies of many saints and martyrs to churches inside the city. There are five major catacombs in Rome today.

SAINT REBECCA

Patroness of a Servant Heart

Feast Day: November 1

Abraham buried his wife Sarah when she died at the age of 127. He himself had reached a ripe old age, and the Lord had blessed him exceedingly. Abraham then called his senior servant, and made him swear that he would not obtain a wife for his son Isaac from the Canaanites, but would instead take him a wife from Abraham's family in Mesopotamia.

Abraham's servant took gifts and traveled to Abraham's birthplace, where he stopped at a well. He asked God that the girl whom He wanted Isaac to marry would give him a drink and water his camels as well. Scarcely had he finished his prayer when Rebekah, the daughter of Abraham's brother Nahor, came to the well with a jug on her shoulder. She was very beautiful, and a virgin. She offered to give a drink to Abraham's servant, and to water his camels as well. Thus he knew that God had favored him. "Then Isaac took Rebekah into his tent; he married her, and thus she became his wife. In his love for her Isaac found solace after the death of his mother Sarah." –GENESIS 24:67

When Rebekah became pregnant with twins, the Lord told her that she was bearing two nations in her womb, and that the older would serve the younger. She gave birth to Esau and Jacob, but preferred Jacob, and helped him obtain Isaac's special blessing. Rebekah died and was buried with Isaac, in the same grave as Abraham and Sarah, the ancestors of Jesus.

SAINT RITA

Patroness of Impossible Cases

Feast Day: May 22

Saint Rita was born at Spoleto, Italy in 1381. At an early age, she begged her parents to allow her to enter a convent; they refused and had her married instead. Rita became a good wife and mother, but her husband was a man of violent temper, who often mistreated his wife. He taught their children his own evil ways. Rita tried to perform her duties faithfully and to pray and receive the sacraments frequently. After nearly 20 years of marriage, her husband was stabbed by an enemy, but before he died, he repented because Rita prayed for him.

Shortly afterwards, Rita's two sons died, and she was alone in the world. Prayer, fasting, penances, and good works filled her days. She was admitted to the convent at Cascia in Umbria, and began a life of perfect obedience and great charity.

Sister Rita had a great devotion to the Passion of Christ. "Please let me suffer like you, Divine Savior," she said one day, and suddenly one of the thorns from the crucifix struck her on the forehead. It left a deep wound which did not heal and which caused her much suffering for the rest of her life. Saint Rita died on May 22, 1457.

Along with Saint Jude, Saint Rita is well-known and loved as the Patron Saint of Lost Causes.

SAINT ROSALIA

Patroness of Palermo, Sicily

Feast Day: September 4

Rosalia, a daughter of a noble family descended from Charlemagne, was born at Palermo in Sicily, and raised around the Sicilian court. Even as a young girl, Rosalia felt God calling he to dedicate her life to Him.

Rosalia went to live in a little room in a cave on Mount Pelegrino, three mile from Palermo, where she offered her heart to God by penance and manual labor, sanctified by assiduous prayer and the constant union c her soul with God.

She wrote on the walls of the cave, "I, Rosalia, daughter of Sinibald, Lord of Roses, and Quisquina, have taken the resolution to live in this cave for the love of my Lord, Jesus Christ." She remained there, hidden from the world, in praye and fasting, living only for and with her Lord. She died alone in 1160.

In 1625, a plague struck Sicily. Saint Rosalia appeared to a hunter near her cave, and he found her body buried in a grotto under the mountain. Her relics were brought to Palermo, and paraded in procession through the streets. The plague ended three days later, and Saint Rosalia was proclaimed patroness of the city. She is known as *La Santuzza* – the Little Saint.

SAINT ROSE PHILIPPINE DUCHESNE

Patroness of Prayer

Feast Day: November 18

ose Philippine Duchesne was born in Grenoble, France, in he French Alps, on August 29, 1769, to Pierre Duchesne and ose Périer. She attended school in the convent of the isitation nuns in Grenoble at the age of 12, and joined them n 1788, to the dismay of her parents, who finally acquiesced.

ose's convent was closed in 1792, due to the Reign of Terror. lthough a laywoman, she established a school for poor hildren, cared for the sick, and hid priests from the evolutionaries. In 1804, Saint Madeline Sophie Barat ncorporated Rose into her Society of the Sacred Heart, nding her and four sisters in 1818 as missionaries to the ouisiana Territory. Rose nearly died due to disease, but she ecovered and went on to establish the first free school west of ne Mississippi River at Saint Charles, Missouri.

lother Duchesne eventually opened six other houses in merica, but her greatest concern was for Native Americans, nd she devoted herself to their education and care. She vangelized the Pottowatomie tribe at age 71, earning from nem the name, *The Woman Who Prays Always.*

aint Rose Philippine Duchesne, a woman of strength, ourage, and passionate faith, died in 1852, at Saint Charles, lissouri, after a decade of retirement in prayer and penance, nd was canonized by Pope John Paul II on July 3, 1988.

SAINT ROSE OF LIMA

Patroness of Florists, Latin America

Feast Day: August 23

The first canonized Saint of the New World was born at Lima, Peru, in 1586. She was christened Isabel, but she was so beautiful that she was called Rose. She became more beautiful as she grew up, and more in love with Jesus, especially in His presence in the Blessed Sacrament.

Rose worked hard to support her poc parents, who wanted her to marry. Rose, however, chose to live a simple life of prayer and penance. She even rubbed pepper on her face so she would not be so attractive.

Rose joined the Dominican Third Order in 1606, at age 20, vowing to live as a virgin. She lived alone in the family garder raising vegetables and serving the poor and sick. A visionary and mystic, Rose suffered physically, emotionally, and spiritually. Yet she would pray, "Lord, increase my sufferings, and with them increase Your love in my heart."

Once pirates attacked Lima, but Rose and the people defeate the enemy by prayer before the Blessed Sacrament.

Saint Rose of Lima died at 31. She stands out for her understanding of the great value of redemptive suffering – offering up our trials for the salvation of others.

SAINT RUTH

Patroness of Loyal Love

Feast Day: November 1

Ruth, a woman from the land of Moab, east of the Jordan, was married to Mahlon, son of Elimelech and Naomi, who had moved to Moab due to a famine in Israel around 1150 BC.

Elimelech and his sons died in Moab and Naomi decided to return to her homeland near Bethlehem. She told Ruth and her other daughter-in-law to return to their families in Moab, marry Moabite men and raise families. Ruth, however, would not leave Naomi. "Do not ask me to abandon or forsake you! For wherever you go I will go, wherever you lodge I will lodge, your people shall be my people, and your God my God. Wherever you die I will die, and there be buried." –RUTH 1:16-17

Naomi and Ruth journeyed to Bethlehem, where Ruth went to work gleaning grain in the field of Boaz, a relative of Elimelech. Boaz took an interest in Ruth, and told her to glean only in his fields, where he would leave extra grain for her. When Ruth asked Boaz why he favored her, a foreigner, he told her that he knew all about what she had done for Naomi, and he prayed that the Lord would reward her.

At the end of the barley and wheat season, Boaz celebrated with an overnight party at the threshing floor. Naomi told Ruth to asked Boaz to cover her with his cloak, as a sign of his protection. Boaz did so, and married Ruth. Their son, Obed, was the grandfather of King David, the ancestor of Jesus.

SAINT SARAH

Mother of the Hebrew People

Feast Day: November 1

Abram married Sarai in the land of Ur, in modern day Iraq. Sarai was barren, without children. Abram's father, Terah, took Abram and Sarai and his family and left Ur for the land of Canaan. He only got as far as Haran, in modern day Turkey.

When Terah died, God appeared to Abram and told him to leave Haran for a land He would show him, promising to make him a great nation. When Abram and Sarai came to the land of Canaan, the Lord promised to give the land to Abram and his descendants. Abram then journeyed to the Negeb area of southern Palestine, and on into Egypt because of famine.

Abram next journeyed to Bethel, near modern day Jerusalem. The Lord again promised to give the land to Abram and his descendants, and to make them as numerous as the dust of the earth. After some time, the Lord again renewed his promise to Abram, who put his faith in the Lord's promise, even though Sarai was barren. Sarai told Abram to have children through her maid, Hagar, and Hagar bore Abram a son, Ishmael.

When Abram was 99, God again appeared to him, changing his name to Abraham, *father of many nations*, and Sarai's name to Sarah, *princess*. God promised to give Abram a son through Sarah, at which Abraham laughed. Sarah gave birth to Isaac – whose name means laughter – a year later. Sarah died at 127 years old, and Abraham buried her at Hebron.

SAINT SCHOLASTICA

Patroness of Epileptics

Feast Day: February 10

Saint Scholastica, sister of Saint Benedict, consecrated her life to God from her earliest youth. After her brother went to Monte Cassino, where he established his famous monastery, he took up her abode in the neighborhood at Plombariola, where she founded and governed a monastery of nuns, about ive miles from that of Saint Benedict, who, it appears, also directed his sister and her nuns. She visited her brother once a year, and as she was not allowed to enter his monastery, he went in company with some of his brethren to meet her at a house some distance away. These visits were spent in onferring together on spiritual matters.

On one occasion they had passed the time as usual in prayer nd pious conversation and in the evening they sat down to take their reflection. Saint Scholastica begged her brother to remain until the next day. Saint Benedict refused to spend the night outside his monastery. She had recourse to prayer and a furious thunderstorm burst so that neither Saint Benedict nor any of his companions could return home. They spent the night in spiritual conferences. The next morning they parted to meet no more on earth.

Three days later Saint Scholastica died, and her holy brother eheld her soul in a vision as it ascended into heaven. He sent his brethren to bring her body to his monastery and laid it in the tomb he had prepared for himself. She died about the year 543, and Saint Benedict followed her soon after. Saint Scholastica considered by many to be the first Benedictine nun.

SAINT SOFIA

Patroness of Widows

Feast Day: August 1

According to a tradition of the Eastern Church, a woman named Sofia lived in Milan, Italy during the reign of Hadrian (117-138 AD). Sofia had three daughters, named Faith (Pistis), Hope (Elpis), and Love (Agape), whom she brought up in the Christian Faith. After her husband's death, she and her daughters moved to Rome.

The Emperor heard of Sofia and her daughters, and sent his soldiers to arrest them. He first examined Faith, who was twelve years old. He tried flattering her, but she boldly scolde him for his shameless deeds and plots against the Christians. Enraged, Hadrian had his soldiers scourge Faith and pour boiling pitch on her. When she survived unharmed from the torture, he had her beheaded.

Next he took Hope, who was only ten years of age. She also confessed Jesus Christ as Lord and Savior, and Hadrian beat her and threw her into a raging fire. The fire went out when i touched her, and he finally had her put to death by the sword

Finally Hadrian took Love, who was only nine. He threw her into a furnace, but an angel delivered her, so Hadrian finally had her beheaded as well. Sofia rejoiced in her daughters' fait and courage, but missed them greatly. She died three days lat as she grieved at the tombs of her three lovely and faithful daughters.

SAINT SUSANNA

Patroness of Courageous Chastity

Feast Day: August 11

Susanna was born in a noble Roman family, the beautiful daughter of Saint Gabinius and niece of Pope Caius, in the 3rd century. She made a private vow of virginity, consecrating herself to Jesus alone.

Susanna lived in the early part of the reign of the Emperor Diocletian, one of the last Roman tyrants to persecute Christians. Diocletian wanted Susanna to marry his adopted son Maximianus Galerius, but she refused, not wanting to marry a man responsible for the deaths of so many believers, and choosing instead to live chastely for Christ.

Diocletian sent two of his court officers, Susanna's uncles Maximus and Claudius, to persuade Susanna to do his will, but she converted them by her piety and holiness. Enraged, Diocletian sent a favorite emissary, Julian, to deal with Susanna. Julian ordered Maximus, Claudius and his wife Praepedigna, and their two sons, to be burned to death at Cumae. Julian exposed Susanna as a Christian, and had her beaten. Finally, he beheaded Susanna and her father at their home in Rome in 295. Emperor Diocletian's wife, Prisca, a secret Christian, buried Susanna covertly, and Susanna's home became the original church that bears her name. Today Santa Susanna's basilica still stands in Rome, a monument to this woman of courage, faith, and true love.

SAINT SYLVIA

Patroness of Safe Delivery for Pregnant Women

Feast Day: November 5

Saint Sylvia, the mother of Pope Saint Gregory the Great, one of the great Doctors of the Church, was born sometime around 520 AD, most likely near the region of Sicily. She was apparently from a distinguished family, as was her husband, the Roman Senator Gordianus, who became one of the seven deacons of Rome. The Church venerates the holiness of Sylvia and Gordianus, as well as Gregory's two aunts, Saints Tarsilla and Emiliana.

Sylvia and her husband had two sons, Gregory and another one whose name has been lost in history. Sylvia gave her sons an excellent Latin education, and after the death of Gordianus in 573, she devoted herself completely to Christ and the Church.

After his father's death, Gregory converted his home in Rome and Sicilian properties into monasteries. Sylvia then retired to live a solitary, monastic type of life in a little home near the church of Saint Sava in Rome. She would send her son fresh vegetables every day on a silver platter, which Gregory one day gave to a poor beggar.

Sylvia died around 592. After her death, Pope Gregory had a mosaic done of his parents which he hung in the church of Saint Andrew in Rome. In the 16th century, Pope Clement VIII inscribed Saint Sylvia in the Roman Martyrology.

SAINT TERESA OF AVILA

Patroness of Headache Sufferers

Feast Day: October 15

When a child of seven years, Teresa ran
away from her home at Avila in Spain,
n the hope of being martyred by the
Moors. Being brought back and asked
he reason of her flight, she replied, "I
vant to see God, and I must die before
can see Him." She then began with
ner brother to build a hermitage in the
garden, and was often heard repeating
Forever, forever."

Some years later Teresa became a Carmelite nun. Frivolous
onversations checked her progress towards perfection, but at
ast, in her 31st year, she gave herself wholly to God. A vision
howed her the very place in hell to which her own light faults
vould have led her, and she lived ever after in the deepest
listrust of self.

Teresa was called to reform her Order, favored with distinct
ommands from Our Lord, and her heart was pierced with
livine love; but she dreaded nothing so much as delusion, and
o the last acted only under obedience to her confessors, which
oth made her strong and kept her safe. Saint Teresa of Avila
lied on October 4, 1582.

et nothing disturb you, let nothing make you afraid.
All things pass away. God never changes.
Patience obtains everything. God alone is enough.

—Saint Teresa of Avila

SAINT TERESA BENEDICTA OF THE CROSS EDITH STEIN

Co-Patroness of Europe

Feast Day: August 9

Edith Stein was born in 1891, the youngest child of a large Jewish family in Poland. At the age of 13, she lost her faith in Judaism. Edith loved learning, and was a brilliant student o philosophy at the University of Gottingen. After reading an autobiography of Saint Teresa of Avila Edith sought to know Jesus, and was baptized at the age of 29 in Cologne, Germany.

In 1934, Edith entered the Carmelite Monastery, taking the name Teresa Benedicta of the Cross. Due to the growing threat of Nazism, she was smuggled out of Germany to Holland in 1938. When the Nazis invaded Holland, Teresa and her sister Rose were arrested and sent to the Auschwitz concentration camp.

Teresa and Rose died in the gas chambers of Auschwitz in 1942. At her beatification in 1987, Pope John Paul II said that the Church honored "a daughter of Israel, who, as a Catholic during Nazi persecution, remained faithful to the crucified Lord Jesus Christ and, as a Jew, to her people in loving faithfulness." Pope John Paul II canonized Saint Teresa Benedicta of the Cross on October 11, 1998.

BLESSED TERESA OF CALCUTTA

Patroness of the Poorest of the Poor

Feast Day: September 5

Agnes Gonxha Bojaxhiu was born August 26, 1910, in Skopje, Macedonia (Albania). The youngest of three children, Agnes felt at an early age the call to help others. Through a parish youth group, she became interested in missionaries. At age 17, she joined the Loreto Sisters of Dublin, known for their work in India. She took the name Teresa, after Saint Therese of Lisieux, Patroness of Missionaries.

In 1929 Sister Teresa arrived in Calcutta to teach at Saint Mary's High School, and in 1944 became principal. In 1946, on a train to Darjeeling, she received "the call within the call," an interior command from Jesus to serve Him in the "poorest of the poor."

In 1948, Pope Pius XII granted Sister Teresa permission to leave her order; she began a school in the Calcutta slums and treated the sick. A few former pupils joined her and in 1950 she founded the Missionaries of Charity.

In 1952 Mother Teresa opened her first Home for the Dying. Her Missionaries of Charity grew from 12 to 4,000 members serving Christ in "the distressing disguise of the poor"–in orphanages, AIDS hospices, and homes for drug addicts, prostitutes and the needy around the world. After suffering greatly from heart and lung illnesses, Mother Teresa died September 5, 1997.

SAINT THERESE OF LISIEUX

Co-Patroness of the Missions

Feast Day: October 1

Therese Martin was born in Alencon, France, in 1873. She was a happy, deeply loved child who loved Jesus as well. Her beloved mother died of breast cancer when Therese was four. Therese herself became so ill with a fever that people thought she was dying. Therese prayed to Mary, who smiled at her and suddenly, she was cured. Therese later said, "Mary is more Mother than Queen."

At the age of 13, Therese greatly desired to join the Carmelites like her sisters Pauline and Marie. However, she was too young, so on a pilgrimage to Rome with her beloved Papa, Therese knelt before Pope Leo XIII and boldly asked his permission. Smiling, Pope Leo said she must obey the bishop, who a short time later allowed her entrance.

Therese offered the rest of her life in prayer and sacrifice for the salvation and sanctification of others, especially priests. Loving and trusting in God, as a child, was her "little way." Her motto was, "Love is repaid by love alone."

Saint Therese died at 24, promising to spend her heaven doing good on earth. Her promised "shower of roses" began and has become a torrent in the Church ever since.

SAINT MOTHER THEODORE GUÉRIN

Patroness of Pioneer Religious

Feast Day: May 14

Anne-Thérèse Guérin was born October 2, 1798, in a fishing village in Brittany, France. Her family's life was hattered when bandits murdered her ather while Anne-Thérèse was still a eenager.

After caring for her family, Anne-Thérèse entered the Sisters of Providence of Ruillé, France, at the age of 25, taking the name Sister Saint Theodore. Though plagued with a chronic stomach illness, ister Theodore served as a teacher of the young and helper of he sick. Then, on July 27, 1840, her superior sent Sister Theodore and four other sisters to America to help found a new community.

On July 4, 1841, the sisters established the Academy of Saint Mary-of-the-Woods at Terre Haute, Indiana, the first Catholic women's liberal arts college in the United States. Mother Theodore went on to establish schools at Jasper, Evansville, nd a number of other towns in Indiana. She also founded wo orphanages in Vincennes, as well as pharmacies in Vincennes and Saint Mary-of-the-Woods.

Mother Guerin died on May 14, 1856. Pope Benedict XVI anonized Saint Mother Theodore Guérin, the eighth saint om the United States, on October 15, 2006. Her tombstone t the motherhouse proclaims: "I sleep, but my heart watches ver this house which I have built."

SAINT VERONICA

Patroness of Photographers

Feast Day: July 12

Saint Veronica is, in tradition, the woman of Jerusalem who wiped the face of Jesus with a veil while He carried His cross on the way to Calvary. According to tradition, the cloth was imprinted with the image of Christ's face. Unfortunately, ther is no historical evidence or scriptural reference for this event, but the story of Veronica became one of the most popular in Christian lore and her veil one of the most beloved relics in the Church.

According to the story, Veronica bore the relic away from the Holy Land, and used it to cure Emperor Tiberius of some illness. The veil was subsequently seen in Rome in the eighth century, and was brought to Saint Peter's in 1297 by comman of Pope Boniface VIII.

Nothing is known about Veronica, although the apocryphal Acts of Pilate identify her with the woman mentioned in the Gospel of Matthew who suffered from an issue of blood. Her name is probably derived from 'vera icon', meaning 'true image'. The term was thus a convenient appellation to denote the genuine relic of Veronica's veil and so differentiate it fron the other similar relics, such as those kept in Milan.

The relic is still preserved in Saint Peter's Basilica, and the memory of Veronica's act of charity is commemorated in the Stations of the Cross. She is honored with a feast day. Her symbol is the veil bearing the face of Christ and the Crown o Thorns.

SAINT VICTORIA

Patroness of True Conviction

Feast Day: December 23

According to tradition, Saint Victoria was a beautiful Christian noblewoman. Her parents had arranged marriages for her and her sister, Saint Anatolia, to Roman pagans named Eugenius and Titus Aurelius. Victoria believed that the marriages would be all right, since the patriarchs in the Old Testament were married. Anatolia argued that those who would live holiest lives should devote themselves wholeheartedly to God and remain single. She said she had seen a vision in which she was told, “Virginity is an immense treasure of the King of kings.”

In the end, Anatolia persuaded Victoria to break off her engagement and consecrate herself completely God. When Eugenius and Titus heard of this, they denounced the women as Christians and obtained authority to imprison them in their estates. When the women converted those sent to guard them, Titus Aurelius gave up. Eugenius kept on, attempting to starve Victoria into submission.

Victoria remained firm in her faith and conviction, and so Eugenius sent her to Julian, the prefect of Rome, who had Victoria beheaded for her faith. Later, Anatolia also suffered martyrdom by the sword during the reign of the Emperor Decius around 250 AD.

SAINT ZITA

Patroness of Domestic Workers

Feast Day: April 27

Zita was born in 1218 at Monte Sagrati, Italy. At 12, she left her home to work as a housekeeper for Pagano Fratinelli and his family, who were wool dealers in the nearby town of Lucca and she stayed there until her death 48 years later. The other servants immediately disliked Zita for her hard work and piety She said, "A servant is not holy if she is not busy." When they saw her giving away food to the poor, they liked her even less and some grew jealous of Zita. However, in time she won over both her employers and her fellow workers by her patience, kindness, and goodness.

Zita went to Mass daily, prayed much, and ministered to the poor and suffering all her life. She had a special regard for criminals in prisons, and cared for them in their need. God worked miracles through Zita, and the news of her good deeds and heavenly visions spread rapidly in the region.

One Christmas Eve, Mr. Fratinelli gave Zita his fur coat because of the bitter cold. As she entered the church, she saw a poor man nearly blue with the cold. She placed the warm covering on his shoulders, telling him to keep it until the end of Mass. After Mass, he was gone. A saddened Zita hurried home to find a stranger at the door, who presented her the coat and disappeared – an angel from heaven!

People sought Zita out, and proclaimed her a saint at her death. Saint Zita was canonized in 1696.

SAINT ZOE

Patroness of Christian Mothers

Feast Day: May 2

ɔe was the wife of Exsuperius, also known as Hesperus. She ıd her husband were both Christians who lived during the ign of Emperor Hadrian, who ruled Rome from 117 to 138 D.

ɔe and her husband and two children, Cyriac and ıeodulus, were slaves to a rich pagan named Catulus, who ved in Pamphylia near the southern coast of modern day ırkey. Catulus was a devout worshiper of the ancient Roman ds. Zoe's job was to take care of the housedogs and keep em from biting visitors! Exsuperius worked out in the fields r from the house, so she seldom saw him. Zoe would often are her own bit of food with the poor people who roamed e roads in those days.

ne day there was a great feast in honor of one of the pagan ds. Catulus roasted some meat and offered it to the gods, d gave it to Zoe and her husband to eat. Zoe and Exsuperius fused to eat it and fed it instead to the dogs.

ıtulus flew into a rage and he took their children and rtured them. Zoe and Exsuperius remained strong in faith d continued to proclaim Jesus as their Lord, Savior, and eliverer. Catulus then cast the whole family into a fiery rnace. Saints Zoe and Exsuperius, Cyriac and Theodulus, rrendered their spirits to the Lord, and died as martyrs.

MARY, QUEEN OF ALL SAINTS

God created us to be His family! When we broke that relationship in the Garden of Eden, God restored it by sending His only Son, “born of a woman.” (GALATIANS 4:4)

God gave Jesus to us through Mary, and Jesus gave Mary to us through John, His beloved apostle, at the foot of the Cross. Mary, the first of all the disciples, supported, guided, and prayed with the apostles after Jesus’ ascension and interceded with them for the gift of the Holy Spirit and abundant supernatural graces poured out at Pentecost.

Mary was and always will be the wellspring for every apostolate. Every saint lives out certain aspects of the gospel; Mary lived them all. She alone is full of grace, and we draw from her abundance. “For he has looked upon his handmaid’s lowliness; / behold, from now on will all ages call me blessed.” (LUKE 1:48)

Mary is the Queen of all saints because she cooperated most faithfully with all the rich graces God granted her. Because of her fullness of grace and splendor of virtues, Mary is raised above all saints as Queen. From Saint Anne to Saint Zoe, a common trait of all saints and heroes of our faith is their devotion to Mary, the mother of Jesus.

O Mary, Queen of All Saints, pray for us!